YALE SCHOOL OF ARCHITECTURE

YALE SCHOOL OF ARCHITECTURE
EDWARD P. BASS DISTINGUISHED VISITING ARCHITECTURE FELLOWSHIP
URBAN INTEGRATION: BISHOPSGATE GOODS YARD NICK JOHNSON / FAT ARCHITECTS

Edited by Nina Rappaport, Andrei Harwell, and Lydia Miller

Yale School of Architecture
180 York Street
New Haven, Connecticut 06520
www.architecture.yale.edu

Distributed by
W. W. Norton & Company Inc.
500 Fifth Avenue
New York, New York 10110
www.wwnorton.com

This book was made possible through the Edward P. Bass Distinguished
Visiting Architecture Fellowship Fund of the Yale School of Architecture.
It is the fourth in a series of publications of the Bass Fellowship published
through the dean's office.

Edited by Nina Rappaport, with Andrei Harwell, and Lydia Miller

Design: mgmt. design, Brooklyn, New York.

Cover: Christopher Corbett

Library of Congress Cataloging-in-Publication Data

Urban integration : Bishopsgate Goods Yard : Nick Johnson/FAT architects /
edited by Nina Rappaport, Andrei Harwell, and Lydia Miller.

p. cm. – (Edward P. Bass distinguished visiting architecture fellowship ; 4
Includes bibliographical references and index.

ISBN 978-0-393-73322-8 (pbk. : alk. paper)

1. Architecture–England–London–History–21st century–Designs and plans.
2. Architecture–Study and teaching–Connecticut–New Haven. 3. Bishopsgate
(London, England)–Buildings, structures, etc.–Designs and plans. 4. London
(England)–Buildings, structures, etc.–Designs and plans. I. Johnson, Nick. II.
Rappaport, Nina. III. Harwell, Andrei. IV. Miller, Lydia. V. FAT (Architectural firm)
VI. Yale University. School of Architecture.

NA970.U73 2010

720.9421–dc22

2010005403

CONTENTS

Edward P. Bass Distinguished Visiting Architecture Fellowship In 2003, Edward P. Bass, a 1967 graduate of Yale College who studied at the Yale School of Architecture as a member of the class of 1972, endowed this fellowship to bring property developers to the school to lead advanced studios in collaboration with design faculty. Mr. Bass is an environmentalist who sponsored the Biosphere 2 development in Oracle, Arizona, in 1991, and a developer responsible for the ongoing revitalization of the downtown portion of Fort Worth, Texas, where his Sundance Square, combining restoration with new construction, has transformed a moribund urban core into a vibrant regional center. In all his work, Mr. Bass has been guided by the conviction that architecture is a socially engaged art operating at the intersection of grand visions and everyday realities.

The Bass fellowship ensures the school curriculum recognizes the role of the property developer as an integral part of the design process. The fellowship brings developers to Yale to work side by side with educators and architecture students in the studio, situating the discussion about architecture in the wider discourse of contemporary practice. In 2005, the first Bass studio, led by Gerald Hines and Stefan Behnisch, Louis I. Kahn Visiting Professor, was documented in *Poetry, Property, and Place* (2006). The second Bass studio, in 2006, teaming Stuart Lipton with Saarinen Visiting Professor Richard Rogers ('62), engineer Chris Wise, and architect Malcolm Smith ('97), was documented in *Future-Proofing* (2007). *The Human City* (2008) records the collaboration of Roger Madelin and Bishop Visiting Professor Demetri Porphyrios. It is a pleasure to see the Nick Johnson and FAT architecture partnership now collected together as *Urban Integration: Bishopsgate Goods Yard*.

Preface: Robert A. M. Stern, Dean *Urban Integration: Bishopsgate Goods Yard* documents the fourth architect-developer studio to be conducted at Yale, led in spring 2008 by Bass Distinguished Visiting Fellow Nick Johnson of Urban Splash and Louis I. Kahn Visiting Assistant Professors of Architecture Sam Jacob, Sean Griffiths, and Charles Holland, partners in the firm FAT (Fashion, Architecture, Taste). Working together with advanced students in architecture, Johnson and FAT considered the history and future of London's Bishopsgate Goods Yard, a significant brownfield site redolent with Victorian associations that is earmarked for redevelopment.

Johnson, a graduate of Sheffield Hallam University from which he holds a bachelor of science in urban land economics, has worked with Urban Splash, the Manchester, England, property developers, for over twelve years, first as a consultant and subsequently as a director. He is responsible for more than £300m of development projects, including Manchester's 3rd Millennium Community; there he is working with various architects including Will Alsop, Foster + Partners, and FAT. Since 2002 Johnson has been a member of the Commission for Architecture and the Built Environment (CABE) and chairman of Marketing Manchester, the agency responsible for worldwide promotion of the city and its region.

The London-based FAT architects concentrates on projects for public and private ventures including, with Urban Splash, the redevelopment of the site of a former public housing development in the New Islington section of Manchester. They also have completed a pavilion in Liverpool, a park and community center in Hoogvliet the Netherlands, and an eighty-unit apartment building in Middlesborough, England. FAT received the Architecture Foundation's New Generation Award 2006 and two RIBA European Awards.

To FAT and Nick Johnson I offer my great appreciation for their dedication to the studio and our students, and I salute the students who so productively and enthusiastically worked together to significantly combine research and design. I also offer thanks to Nina Rappaport, publications director at the Yale School of Architecture, who with Andrei Harwell (M. Arch, 2006) assistant to the studio, and Lydia Miller (M. Arch, 2008), one of the students in the studio, helped structure *Urban Integration* and see it through to publication as the fourth book in this series documenting the work of the Edward P. Bass Distinguished Visiting Architecture Fellowship.

Introduction: Nina Rappaport, Andrei Harwell and Lydia Miller Developer Nick Johnson and FAT architects have worked together before. That collaboration inspired the organization of their studio at Yale incorporating intensive research and planning for the redevelopment of an urban area in London. The first section of the book, "Beyond Design: Placemaking and the City," features interviews with Nick Johnson and the three FAT partners the Louis I. Kahn Visiting Assistant Professors, Sam Jacob, Sean Griffiths, and Charles Holland. The second section, "Regenerating Bishopsgate Goods Yard," places the site and the program in the context of contemporary London with essays by architectural critic Kieran Long, D'Arcy Fenton, architect with Foster + Partners, and John McMorrough, assistant professor at the Knowlton School of Architecture at Ohio State University. "Bishopsgate Goods Yard Studio Work," the last section, begins with the studio brief and continues with the studio exercises, student planning analyses, and the students' final project designs.

For the first half of the semester the students tackled preliminary exercises to explore creative ideas for understanding the site and issues. The assignments, represented in the section "Framework Design Exercises," included, *x100*, in which the students designed an object one hundred times; *People in Architecture*, which raised questions about how architecture should be represented, included vignettes of activities; and *3 into 1*, which sought hybrid design solutions by combining disparate precedents utilizing various representational techniques, from overlay to folding. Nick Johnson helped students understand how questions of economic viability might work for or against each of their projects and kept the projects grounded, asking questions about the character of the places they were designing, and what it would actually be like to visit or live there.

Much of the studio work was a response to the existing conditions of the site and looked for an alternative to the 2007 development proposal by Hammersons with architects Foster + Partners. In the "Regenerating Bishops Gate Goods Yard" section D'Arcy Fenton, a partner at Foster, describes the challenges of developing the site. Throughout the studio, emphasis was placed on using various drawing techniques and multimedia to represent the diverse communities, along with more traditional plan and elevation drawings. After the students visited the site and understood the complex context, they expanded on the experience of the first exercise to rapidly design one hundred schemes for the site over two days. For midterm, the students divided into pairs to complete an urban "master vision."

During the semester's second half, students refined their urban concepts, by developing one portion of their scheme in more detail. Final projects were charged with the responsibility of creating new and interesting dynamics between different kinds of people who might live, work, plan, or create on the site, thus capturing the hybridity and vitality of a city. Student project descriptions and discussion highlights at final reviews before a jury of architects, writers, and professors including, Patrick Bellew, Kieran Long, Frank Lupo, John McMorrough, Emmanuel Petit, Elihu Rubin, Michael Speaks, Frederick Tang, Susan Yelavitch, and Mimi Zeiger, raised additional insights into issues of content and context.

The editors would like to acknowledge the work of the students (all class of 2008) who participated in the studio and whose cooperation was essential to this book: Lasha Brown, Ashima Chitre, Christopher Corbett, Chiemeka Ejiochi, Gabrielle Ho, Elizabeth McDonald, Nicholas McDermott, Christina Wu, and Shelley Zhang. We would also like to extend thanks to our copy editor, David Delp, and graphic designer, Sarah Gephart of mgmt. design, in New York.

I. BEYOND PLACEMAK AND THE CI

DESIGN:
NG
TY

EYOND
PLACEMAK
AND THE CI

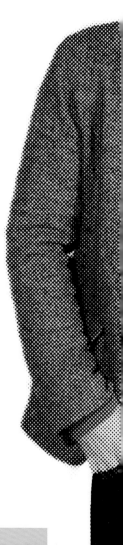

Nick Johnson, director of Urban Splash

FAT architects, from left: Charles Holland, Sean Griffiths, and Sam Jacob

Nick Johnson, director of Urban Splash was interviewed by Nina Rappaport about his role as developer and civic booster.

Nina Rappaport: The interests and goals of younger developers seem to focus more on design and making cities vibrant places than on cookie-cutter commercial projects. How has the younger generation of developers made an impact on the selection of architects in property development? How do you work with architects in general?

Nick Johnson: I think clients are now more design-literate and adventurous; and a younger architectural practice in England can get commissions from invited competitions—in which there is a chance to compete on a level playing field—because the entries are anonymous and not prejudged. They never even consider what it feels like to stand where they have just drawn a line. Their ability to impose rather than celebrate living is harsh. Some architects will corrupt function purely for aesthetic satisfaction, and that really irritates me. As the client, you aren't locked into any particular style. I consider architecture to be a bit like a record collection. You don't listen to the same artists or genre all the time. People have very eclectic music collections. The privilege of being a client is the ability to deliver that mixture and not only commision a particular style or genre of architecture—for example, I would say New Islington, in Manchester, is my record collection.

NR: New Islington is diverse stylistically because you broke away from your earlier projects, which were smaller, more "stylish" loft developments, to expand toward creating a mixed-use and variable-income community. When does good design turn a profit, and how did you switch from being a residential developer to designing entire communities and regeneration projects?

Nick Johnson: The traditional adage in the 1980s was that good design costs money, and we grew up through the punk era of the late 1970s and the nightclubs of the 1980s, with visual references from the likes of Neville Brody and *Face* magazine. It was the age of design consciousness; fashion became a part of everyday life. Objects started to be packaged and designed well, so we became more design-literate. Design was seen in the more ephemeral, the less permanent, arts rather than in the built environment; it was in furniture and graphic design. We believed our first step was that good architectural design adds value to buildings rather than just to the expense. That philosophy stood us in good stead for five years. But the ability to pick a good architect to come up with a good solution gets boring, quite frankly, and it was apparent that more people were catching up with us. In the late 1990s the agenda was beginning to shift politically, and we moved from the "scorched-earth policy" of Thatcherism and belief in the market; we started to move toward a socially

Sean Griffiths, Sam Jacob, and Charles Holland, partners in FAT, met with Nina Rappaport to discuss their work and approach to urban design as well as their Yale studio project.

Nina Rappaport: I have heard Bob Venturi likes your work and writings. Have you used his work as a basis from which to project your own ideas? How did you come to reassess Post-Modern architecture, and where has it led you?

Sean Griffiths: I wrote a review in the *RIBA Journal* a few years ago of the exhibition *Out of the Ordinary,* in Philadelphia, saying I thought Venturi and Scott Brown were extremely misunderstood in Great Britain, in that their work was more radical than people thought. When the Prince of Wales intervened in the debate about the National Gallery Extension, they were seen as being conservative imposters, and architects here were weary of their attacks on Modernist orthodoxy. Everybody hated that building, but of course I quite liked it. Venturi wrote a very appreciative letter to me, and I was thrilled. One of the reasons we were interested in them is because they were so unfashionable in the 1990s.

Sam Jacob: We had also—almost by accident—found ourselves in possession of a large library of Post-Modern architecture books. I would pick them up at used bookstores at knock-down prices. Obviously, this kind of architecture was very out of fashion in the 1990s, which is why they were used books. But we started to see something else, something very relevant to the way we were thinking about architecture.

Sean Griffiths: One book was by the artist Dan Graham, whose work I like, such as the altered-glass house with the mirror in the middle, which was a dialogue between a Miesian house and a suburban tract house. Graham's essays about Robert Venturi were different in terms of the attack on the Modernist orthodoxy and how radical it was to expose all those conceits that existed within the Modernist light. Graham saw the work as being parallel to what environmental artists Robert Smithson and Richard Long were doing in the late 1960s. My interest in Venturi was sort of like admitting to liking pornography—something you don't talk about in polite company. Venturi was also interested in the Pop thing, the whole deadpan approach to creation.

Sam Jacob: In Post-Modernism we saw something that seemed open-ended and incredibly relevant. Its interest in communication and media seemed to resonate with an era in which communication technology was—and still is—transforming the ways we live and work. Equally, Post-Modernism's interest in the everyday seemed to offer a way of engaging political and social issues in a way that late Modernism singularly failed to do. And its insistence, especially in early projects, on an explicit agenda resonated with the kind of work

Urban Splash developer, Will Alsop Partners, CHIPS, New Islington, 2009

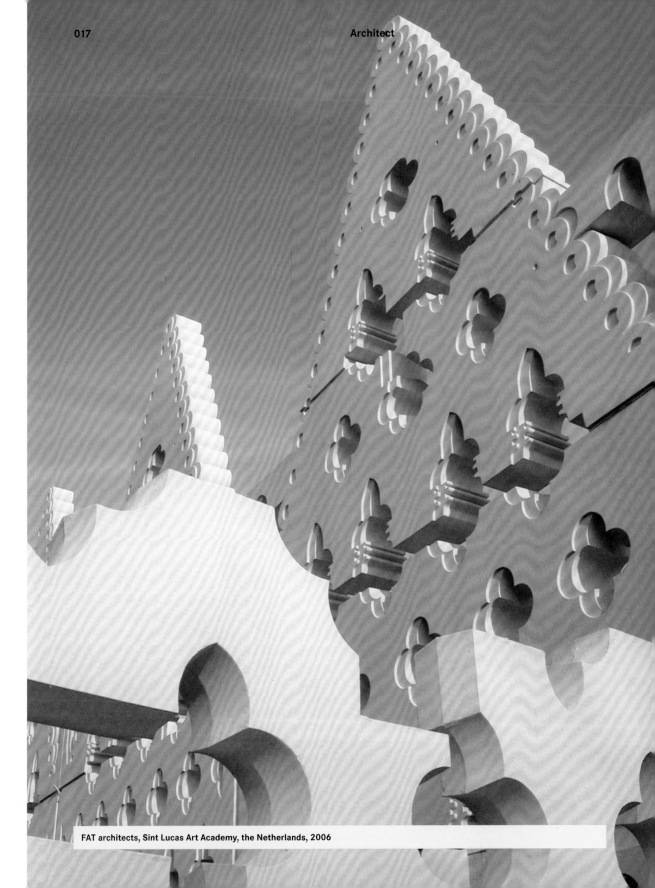

FAT architects, Sint Lucas Art Academy, the Netherlands, 2006

FAT architects, Sint Lucas Art Academy, the Netherlands, 2006

responsible agenda, which then was not just about design but also about mixed-use and vital communities. Thus, we have shifted in the last twelve years from being just a property developer to being a regeneration company for larger sites and communities, with more than 250 employees.

NR: What led you to start to develop large-scale, former industrial sites in downtowns, and how were the developments maintained as mixed in use and income levels?

Nick Johnson: Industrial buildings were cheaper per square foot than carpet at the time, but no one would buy them. We began to explore mixed tenure, which provides a variety of means to buy a home. We likened it to buying a car wherein you decide what car you want to buy first and then which way you will buy it—you can rent it, buy a share, or buy it outright. We also wanted to take the stigmatism out of mixed housing by designing apartment buildings that have a complete mix of tenure, which we called "tenure blind." The affordable-housing element is the same as property available at market value: traditionally, developers would build a block of lower-quality housing at a lower specification at the worst part of the site to discharge obligations to provide it. For our projects, the goal is to not even know how your neighbor bought their house nor whether it is socially subsidized rent.

NR: If you make social issues a part of the moneymaking equation when the standard developers care only about the high-end rental potential for both residential and commercial spaces, how do you subsidize and finance tenants with these various income levels?

Nick Johnson: We work with government agencies that provide funding to allow people to buy into the housing market at the entry level. We also work with housing associations, which have to provide "social rented" accommodation. Embracing the agenda of social issues also results in making more money. Traditionally, the private sector delivered profit without social responsibility. But there is no more socially responsible job than building. It is the most public of art forms. It has the capacity to influence the way people exist in a city and to bestow joy and satisfaction or instill terror and fear in equal measure.

NR: How did the New Islington development project come your way? Why did you want to work on it, and how do you envision it?

Nick Johnson: New Islington was a government initiative formed as a partnership between the Manchester City Council and English Partnership, given impetus by the Millennium Community Initiative, and launched by John Prescott. Our model will show that embracing social responsibility will result in them making more we were doing—the idea that projects for advertising agencies or nightclubs in provincial English towns could have agendas.

Charles Holland: The Venturis were also engaged in the American landscape, looking at the everyday commercial and vernacular landscape in the same way Pop artists were trying to do. They're still not really given any credit for this. They tried to reconcile being high-brow architects with not being exclusive and with genuinely trying to engage with a lived reality. So there is a serious side to our interest in early Post-Modernism, a sense that it was a very interesting and provocative project that then, unfortunately, blew up into this big commercial monster. But the things that Sean and Sam are talking about—Dan Graham, VSBA's studies of Levittown, and so on—these are still really useful things for architects to look at. Of course, the fact that everyone else hates it makes it a guilty pleasure for us!

NR: Do you feel Modernism is not appreciated because it is too conceptual?

Sam Jacob: Quite the opposite. As Modernism lost its capital "M" and became modernism, it jettisoned a conceptual approach—or what we might call an "idea"—and instead pursued a process of formal refinement. Part of the concept, the idea, behind our work is to widen the canon of architectural language—wide enough that it can comprehend what we might be able to think of as architectural. To that end, we were not interested in only architecture.

Sean Griffiths: We started with street-based art projects in which we were putting radical interventions in familiar spaces like bus shelters, where you are just standing there waiting for a bus, to engage somebody in something. We were interested in communication, how you touch an audience. People in the art and architecture worlds said, "Hey, there is something interesting there." But being contrarian has blighted our careers ever since. We began to ask, what the hell is radical about making some art? What is radical about a bunch of people walking around in black? I come from a working-class background, and I would say that, actually, it is not radical; it is a form of entertainment for the chattering classes, who are a sort of liberal intelligentsia. We had a house project for two writers, and we said, "Let's have a look at what people like Venturi and Charles Moore would do. Let's go to this taboo ground called Post-Modernism." Two levels are legible: On the one hand, you can be an architectural aficionado and see historic references in our Blue House, in Bethnal Green, but somebody walking by on a wet Sunday morning might say, "Cute house," and smile, and it lifts their spirits for five seconds and maybe adds three weeks to their life.

Urban Splash developer, Will Alsop Partners, CHIPS, New Islington, 2009

money. The council estate in Manchester was arguably the most deprived in the city, with the ring road around it and a 1980s shopping mall perched on the edge, which cut off the city. We were selected as a developer in a competition based on our philosophical approach and track record rather than an actual scheme, which is liberating. We worked with the residents to choose the architects for the master plan and short-listed the practices: Rogers, Arup, Ian Simpson, Eric von Egerat, and Will Alsop. A defining moment in the transition of my view about architecture was when we asked Alsop about what council estate might be and what were the opportunities for it, he made us laugh and talked about wonder, delight, and fun, whereas the other architects were overly professional and incredibly boring.

NR: How is Alsop's new building, CHIPS, being received by the general public and development groups, and who are the new residents?

Nick Johnson: I was really pleased to be approached the other night by Elliot Rashman, the man behind the music group Simply Red's management company, who said he thought it was the only true iconic building in Manchester and the best building we've ever done. I'm also pleased to say there are also people who hate it. Precisely just the way it should be. You can't be ambivalent about CHIPS.

I'm now living in the building, which is the first Alsop residential building in the U.K. The new residents are a mix of families (like mine) and young people who are getting their first home. The problem is that the rest of the buildings are likely to be delivered over a much longer time period as a result of what has happened in the global economy.

NR: Since Manchester had only a small residential population even in the Industrial Revolution, how do you bring people into the heart of the city to live? What is its new identity? Your role as chairman of the Manchester Marketing Group must naturally integrate with attracting people to buy your properties.

Nick Johnson: This chairmanship came about in rather an odd and typically Manchester way. Ten years ago I chaired the "anti" Manchester Marketing Group, the McEnroe Group, to respond to its campaign to market the city with the tagline "We're up and going," which came about after the IRA bomb blew the heart out of the city. We described it as "mediocrity at its most mediocre" and brought about the downfall of the organization. Ten years on they appointed me as chairman, and I'm responsible for establishing a new strategic direction for the organization, which will focus around the work of graphic artist Peter Saville, who has proposed a new tagline, "Manchester. Original. Modern." Peter, Tony Wilson [founder of Factory Records

NR: Early Post-Modernism was often a commentary on Modern architecture and society, but then it got absorbed as a style. Are you trying to go back to that transition point? Is your approach primarily intellectual or playful?

Sean Griffiths: I think it's a bit of both; we don't use the word *Post-Modernism* much because it is an automatic label. If our work has a relationship with anything, it is linked to the Post-Modernism of the 1960s and 1970s, not the bastardized 1980s stuff, as you just said. There is a cycle of making an interesting beginning to something that becomes compromised, which is found not only in Post-Modernism but also in mid-century Modernism today.

NR: Even your name—FAT (Fashion, Architecture, Taste)—is a bit irreverent. I remember first seeing your website and the discussion around this alternative architecture firm that was making fun of architects. But your architecture wasn't known at all in the United States, or maybe there wasn't any here yet to speak about?

Charles Holland: Architecture is a profession, and as such it has to appear much more sensible than, for instance, art. Architects want to give the impression of being professional advisers to the client knowledgeable about net-to-gross ratios and so on, and so irreverence, wit, and humor are in short supply. What people see as our irreverence or humor is partly a critical position that explores the latent desires behind what architects actually do. Take the issue of taste. Architects never talk about taste, but it's a huge consideration behind what they do. We are interested in how taste dictates architectural production, and so we design things that are provocative in that sense. This approach makes it appear irreverent and certainly gives it a notoriety among architects. The irreverence can be a problem, of course, especially when it came to the website. What people perceived as silliness has often gotten in the way of the seriousness. I would say the work is extremely serious in intent but has irreverent qualities in the way it is done.

Sam Jacob: Maybe the constant is an idea of content. The name was supposed to be a name for a magazine, but we got only as far as designing the cover and a failed application to the Arts Council, all of which left us with a name and logo. We got known through the website because of the one thing we wrote, "How to Become a Famous Architect," which got e-mailed around to pools of interested friends all over the world. It was a semi-autobiographical story of a ten-step plan, which was later published in *Perspecta 38: Famous*. That got us "famous," which was ironic.

NR: How do you incorporate place and context in the narrative of your work? How does the concept emerge

FAT architects, Hoogvliet Park, the Netherlands, 2006

FAT architects, Hoogvliet Park, the Netherlands, 2006

and the Hacienda Club], and I are big fans of Richard Florida's Pop academic proposition that the liveliness, diversity, and soul of a city influences its future economic success. Punk music, Factory Records, and the Hacienda Nightclub, which is now celebrating its twenty-fifth anniversary, still have a dramatic effect on teenagers. Tony Wilson says the reason the music from Manchester is so strong is the kids have the most eclectic record collections, and so what you hear is a fusion of eclecticism and attitude. Apart from soccer, it is the second-biggest export of the city. That's where the Marketing Manchester thing fits in, and if I do my job correctly, we should be able to have an influence on all aspects of wealth generation.

NR: On top of all the social and cultural interests, how do you integrate sustainability into large-scale projects? Is it through the infrastructure or the individual architectural units, in terms of design or the organizational structure of a site?

Nick Johnson: Environmental responsibility should be integrated so that the only lifestyle choice required from purchasers or tenants is household recycling; the rest should be done by us. We should be using all our creative capital to make what we do better for the planet. We're just in the process of establishing our own utility company to control the way in which energy is generated to ensure that it's as environmentally responsible as possible. We're going to generate energy locally from combined heat-and-power units, which have the capacity to generate up to fifty percent of the peak electrical load and all the heating and cooling on a site. Once we become part of the energy supply chain to our developments, which I see as a natural progression, then we become much more interested in how much energy our apartments and office buildings consume.

NR: How are you combining revitalization with sustainability in the renovation of the former tobacco company building, Lakeshore, into a residential complex?

Nick Johnson: The redevelopment of Lakeshore was a victim of the credit crunch, but we're just in the process of securing public-sector investment that will get us to completion. But it's very unlikely there will be funding after that for the foreseeable future. We're happy we'll be busy for the next couple of years working on these projects, and in the meantime we just have to figure out a way of delivery to suit the new economic paradigm. The objectives are still the right objectives—great places in "proper" communities.

NR: If cities are constantly changing places in terms of population, development, and activities, where in a project can you anticipate change and build in flexibility, what the 2006 Edward P. Bass developer/architect studio called "future-proofing"?

from the place, rather than being imposed from the outside? For example, your New Islington project for Urban Splash was a community-based project.

Sam Jacob: In a sense, we see context as a narrative more than a physical condition. Historical reference, social issues, and the contemporary tensions of a site become a narrative arc that allows us to speculate on the future of a site. It is an attempt to understand the different forces at work on a place and to articulate, explore, or speculate on how these tensions might create a design approach.

Charles Holland: Going back to Venturi's *Complexity and Contradiction,* I always liked the idea of two things that are oppositional and incongruous coming together, which seems to be a true representation of what life is like. Formal juxtaposition plays a big part in what we do. The Tanner Point Housing project was about reinventing an idea for the vertical city through a specific response to the East End of London, which has huge ethnic and social diversity and is short on family housing. We are adapting the standard apartment block to demonstrate how you can accommodate five-bedroom units along one side, so there is a core in the middle and half of the block would be one apartment. You would put a big balcony along the back where a kid could ride a bicycle up and down, and you could build in a certain amount of adaptability to give residents a say in the design.

NR: Do you see your approach to these housing projects as more utopian or pragmatic?

Sean Griffiths: Utopian projects are very difficult in today's culture, even if one wanted to do them. In a culture driven by a vision of diversity, one might think of our approach as a utopia wherein everyone is happy together regardless of race, class, and so on. Now there is a certain kind of utopian vision emerging from the environmental movement, which is a vision promoted in particular in this city.

Charles Holland: Our projects are, inevitably, a mixture. Something like Islington Square is certainly utopian in a sense; we were trying to make the best possible new houses we could and also make something utterly new. At the same time, they don't look utopian in the conventional architectural manner, and they reflect some very non-utopian things about how people live and organize their houses. It depends on your definition of "utopian," really, and in architecture that tends to be a certain "look" that echoes the utopian projects of the past. Our approach is not utopian in a tabula rasa sense of sweeping away convention and replacing it with a singular architectural vision. But I think it continues aspects of the social and cultural ambitions of early Modernist utopianism.

Urban Splash, park in New Islington, 2009

Nick Johnson: The key is to create a flexible framework rather than a prescriptive master plan. I even said at a recent lecture for CABE, "Ban the master plan." At New Islington we called it a "strategic framework plan," but more important were the five key moves and the establishment of a "tone" that would allow each architect to interpret in his or her own way. New Islington is a twelve-year program, so flexible frameworks are essential to responding to societal changes over time.

NR: The process to choose FAT as the architect for one section of the Methodist Housing Association residential development was an interesting one for Urban Splash. Why were they selected as the architect? Now that their housing units are built, how has it worked out in terms of financial and community success?

Nick Johnson: The residents worked with us on all decisions, including the selection of Alsop and FAT. We ran a competition with RIBA in which the brief implied we were a client interested in architectural adventure and expressed the residents' desire to build what they already have, since they were being relocated. We were looking for a practice that could articulate the apparent friction between our wider aspirations for design, but we didn't want compromise. We downplayed the opportunity to manage the architect's expectations. Some were put off by that, but FAT wasn't. The residents asked dead-simple but unnerving questions of the architects, which showed how much they had learned in the community workshop process. One reason FAT was chosen was that they were fun and relaxed, and they made everyone comfortable. The residents weren't that interested stylistically into what it would look like—they just wanted a new home. We were delighted our first competition was won by the agent provocateur FAT. This goes back to the record-collection idea: they were the wild card at the opposite end of the spectrum from the slick Modernism that we are known for, taking us into a different realm and challenging our own set of values about the relevancy of what we are doing. It was an intellectual test for us that I knew would aggravate and provoke the architectural world, especially in Manchester, which is locked into a perceived set of polite, modern contextualism.

NR: Were you concerned with aesthetic considerations in the end?

Nick Johnson: The aesthetic is not irrelevant but very cleverly worked out. You have to be gifted to know how to balance kitsch with the profound and challenge preconceptions about what architecture is and what it should look like. FAT is intelligent enough to get that balance right. You don't read it as kitsch or Post-Modernism but as fun, delight, and surprise.

NR: Do you think architecture needs to be more about pleasure and less about programmatic practicality? How would you incorporate those concepts into an urban design scheme such as the one you hosted for the students at Yale?

Charles Holland: Actually, we think it should be less about pleasure! No one signs up for a solely practical or functional approach. The bigger question is, whose pleasure? For whom is one designing? Our Yale project was about trying to reconcile irreconcilable differences. The assumption of the traditional master plan is that it can describe an inclusive, perfect scenario and, in doing so, assumes a kind of neutrality on the part of the master-planner.

Our brief was about challenging that neutrality, making the master plan recognize conflicting and divergent desires and interests. The area we chose—Bishopsgate Goods Yard—is a very particular site bordered by radically different versions of London: the financial district of the city, the über-fashionable Shoreditch, the Bangladeshi population of Brick Lane, and so on. How do you articulate that in a master plan?

We were also trying to challenge the consensus of current master-planning convention, which is to turn old industrial areas into "cultural quarters"—new landscapes of leisured consumption populated by smiling children and well-heeled parents, with the odd artist around to give it some edge.

NR: What is your approach to urban design and the teaching of urban design? What do you think is the role of the architect in urbanism?

Charles Holland: Our urban design approach follows from the architectural one. It's an attempt to not smooth away difference or create a sort of tasteful Esperanto. We have been involved in a number of master-planning projects lately, including one for expanding the village of Bere Regis, in Dorset.

Urban design today is interesting, partly because any building outside of cities is hugely contentious in the U.K., but also because we are interested in the kinds of spatial organization that would be appropriate. There is a history of spaces just as there is a history of architectural styles or types, and these different spaces have associations and overt meanings as well as form a backdrop for other activities.

Sometimes we use quite different types of organization that can cut across each other to create unexpected spaces and places—ones that might combine, for instance, elements of the village green, the formal square, and the sports field. At Hoogvliet, the Netherlands, we designed a park that combined fragments of many

Urban Splash developer, FAT architects, New Islington housing, Manchester, England, 2006

FAT architects, Urban Splash developer, New Islington housing, Manchester, England, 2006

Urban Splash developer, FAT architects, New Islington Housing, Manchester, England, 2006

different kinds of public space: formal, informal, urban, suburban, functional, romantic, and so on. We did this in order to reflect the genuine conditions of the place, the way people might use the space, so that it was somewhere for parties, barbecues, model-boat enthusiasts, bird watchers, and so on, and to give those different uses some expression. I suppose we are trying to evolve a public language that communicates a genuine complexity and dynamism about spaces. We are interested in combining quite formal and historical architectural and urban types with a more narrative understanding of place that messes up those archetypes.

NR: How do you think your work attracted the interest of property developers such as Nick Johnson, who brings the community into the discussion in developer-led projects? How is development in London becoming more in tune with local residents or perhaps more socially conscious?

Charles Holland: The project we set for the semester was partly about the fact that socially conscious design doesn't really exist. For instance, what is a socially conscious public space? Is it a place where social tensions are expressed rather than smoothed out? "Socially conscious design" suggests somehow resolving social problems, which, again, I don't think we are interested in. We aren't necessarily looking to resolve anything in that sense. We are more interested in the differences and tensions.

Sean Griffiths: I think there are two sides of it. An organization like Urban Splash is not your typical commercial developer. In the last ten years there has been a much greater recognition of the role that architecture can play, so we as architects can debate what good design is. In large regeneration projects, developers can't just come in and buy a piece of land; they have to demonstrate what value they are adding, how they are helping to provide social housing, what are their green credentials, and what other uses and facilities they are providing.

Sam Jacob: Developers like Urban Splash recognize there are young architects who will work very hard to realize a good project—to make their architectural mark. It's an optimistic scenario for young architects, but, equally, developers get a much better product because of what you might call youthful enthusiasm. Developers have become much more sophisticated. You can see this in how they communicate and market their product. Architecture is one way in which they can make a splash, another way of marketing. In this way, for certain kinds of developers, architectural innovation is a means of adding value. This seems to have been the cultural shift in the relationship between developers and architects. So the project we set for the Yale studio was a way of exploring the politics of regeneration from a more critical perspective.

Urban Splash developer, FAT architects, New Islington housing, Manchester, England, 2006

FAT architects, Urban Splash developer, New Islington housing, Manchester, England, 2006

III. REGENE
BISHOPSGA
GOODS YAR

Looking south, the recent construction in the City of London brings increased density and height to the site.

The Braithwait viaduct remains on the southern half of the site as the new subway stop is built to the north.

Current site

Willful Amnesia in Contemporary London Urbanism: Kieran Long Bishopsgate Goods Yard's redevelopment is typical of the confidence and speed that characterized the work of property developers in pre-recession twenty-first-century London. The plans to change this part of east London's urban landscape are emblematic of the ambition and cultural naïveté of urban development in the city and the U.K. generally. They also demonstrate, despite the vogue for large-scale public consultation, the desire of developers and local authorities to ignore evidence from the margins when doing urban design. In the process, developers have created a language for themselves that is deemed acceptable by local authorities and national government but one that seems remote from the lived reality of the city.

The archaeology of undelivered visions and plans for the area may seem faintly amusing during a recession this deep; the quantity of funding required to carry out the project seems like a vision from another time. But a discussion of whether highly leveraged commercial development models are a thing of the past can wait for more qualified commentators than me. For an observer of urban design and architecture, the ongoing attempts to make Bishopsgate Goods Yard into an inhabited part of the city show a familiar oscillation between the visionary and the specific, couched in terms with which it is difficult to disagree.

The local authority, the London Borough of Tower Hamlets, knows the site is a potential jewel in its crown. The corner of this poor borough that touches the financial heart of London was an opportunity to cash in on a seemingly inexorable demand for commercial and residential development. To facilitate this, Bishopsgate was framed as an extension of the city, rather than as an extension of the delightful chaos of Brick Lane, the nineteenth-century social-housing utopia of the Boundary Estate, or the artistic ghetto and the social hub of Shoreditch.

In the process of planning the site, every participant internalized a language that is consummate in its aspirational vagueness. This language could not be further from that of a regular citizen's and is not even very close to the words used by politicians; rather, it is the language of consumerism, of broad measurables. It talks of development, mixed use, community, amenity, public space, opportunity, and density. All these terms find their etymology in urban-design terms deployed in the Urban Task Force Report, the influential document published in 1998 by a team led by Sir Richard Rogers. For instance, the many aspirations about Bishopsgate include talk about high buildings as being somehow part of creating a "world-class" city, as making London a coherent whole, as being closer in spirit to New York, Tokyo, or Shanghai, than any other city in the U.K.

Recent demolition creates a nearly empty site juxtaposed to the density of existing urban fabric.

(Top) Demolition of the upper rail level in an advanced state. The brick wall on the perimeter is a historically listed site. (Bottom) A view of the site in 2007 from the Brick Lane construction entrance showing the extensive clearing of the site in preparation for the expansion of the east London subway line.

KCAP, a well-respected Dutch master-planning office, describes Bishopsgate Goods Yard as "being transformed into a dynamic urban hub." Foster + Partners worked on an Urban Design Framework (UDF) for the site with Anglo-Dutch architect Maccreanor Lavington between 2005 and 2006. A UDF sounds like something that might be a mandatory planning requirement for any site, but it isn't. Nor is a UDF exactly a master plan, although it will often suggest formal proposals for buildings, as well as specify or suggest programs for use and public spaces. Often, more detailed strategies are adopted as so-called Supplementary Planning Guidance by the local authority, which gives the plans formal status.

KCAP's strategy is typical, programmatically led Dutch urbanism, with a series of blocks arranged on top of and around a large plinth, with areas of public space fronted by retail. Like many UDFs carried out by architects in London, it tends toward being detailed and propositional, showing perspectives of potential public spaces and the massing of buildings.

If the proof of a plan's efficacy is how similar the results look to the proposal, UDFs in London have not proven to be very robust. Take Barking, an outlying town center in east London where the Urban Design Framework carried out for the boroughs of Barking and Dagenham (designed by East Architects with Sergison Bates in 2004) was supplemented by another, more detailed plan by architect Allies & Morrison in 2005 and 2006. Today, there are few outcomes in the Barking town center that can be traced directly back to these frameworks or that of other interested parties, including private developers and regional and national development agencies. However, these plans did begin a process of urban change that no single individual has controlled. In a place like Barking, the strategies helped to raise aspirations and begin a debate, but they were not delivered wholesale.

Bishopsgate has a much higher profile and infinitely more commercial potential. The most famous commercial architect in the world, Foster + Partners, was brought in to look at the western end of the site in another attempt to prove the "world-classness" of the plans. The firm is the author of the most popular tall building in London (30 St. Mary Axe, or the Gherkin) and was a logical choice. The selection of this consultant team shows that the developers, Ballymore in partnership with Hammerson, had just enough knowledge of architecture and design to be dangerous. By choosing Foster, the developers can help to neuter objections to the proposal using design grounds from the local authorities or the national design watchdog, Commission for Architecture and the Built Environment (CABE).

It is fascinating how, in such a vibrant and diverse piece of London, the development partners were able to establish Bishopsgate Goods Yard as a tabula rasa with commercial potential, despite local opposition. This process began with the site's classification as a brownfield, a euphemism designed to make any inner city sound ripe for regeneration. Tower Hamlets' recent publication of a new UDF—by Terry Farrell & Partners, released for consultation in February 2009—shows how the idea of Bishopsgate Goods Yard as a blank canvas is completely internalized: "The site is vacant and has been identified in existing planning documents as an opportunity for regeneration," says the document, which elsewhere employs the words *dereliction* and *vacancy*—a language of emptiness. The Farrell & Partners document also spends a lot of time observing the surrounding buildings but hardly any time on the recent history of the site.

It doesn't take a genius to know the site was never exactly vacant; English Heritage's battle to preserve the historic remains of the goods yard is testament to that. Even the demolition and subsequent construction of a new railway station on the site hasn't quite destroyed every physical trace of what was there before.

The analysis in the Farrell & Partners document of what it calls the "historic context" mentions the existing English Heritage–listed railway structures but then reiterates the site has been "derelict" since 1964, "except for temporary uses." While many of those temporary uses—the pet market in the arches on Bethnal Green Road, the flea markets under the viaduct, and myriad art projects by students and others—live vividly in the memories of those who experienced them. Yet, the place's recent forty-five-year period is not considered as being part of the "historic context" and these uses are not described or considered as part of the plan. This exclusion might seem natural, but it is another example of the privileging of nineteenth-century over twentieth-century history in the historic surveying of London.

The report concludes by citing the evidence of two public "drop-in" sessions, held in summer 2008, which discovered "that the vast majority of respondents believe it is unacceptable to leave the site in its current form." In their typical broad stroke, the master planners prove that change is better than no change. This conclusion is extremely useful for the local authorities and prospective developers, who now feel they can hoist change on the public and it will be viewed in a positive light.

The contrasts between the flashiness of Ballymore and Hammerson's plans with the new document are salutary, though. The Farrell & Partners' plan is almost against design, with hideously colored maps captioned in Comic Sans typeface, with a few bad photographs as the only visuals. Perhaps in the document is recognition that design-led master-planning has failed the site. In any case, while the original, commercially led proposals are unlikely to be delivered soon, their legacy will be to allow the erasure of history and culture at this site through the rhetoric of regeneration.

(Top) Bishopsgate Terminus in 1850 from the *Illustrated London News* showing the hustle and bustle of goods and people in the lower levels of the viaduct. (Bottom) Main passenger station entrance on the corner of Shorditch High Street and Commercial Street.

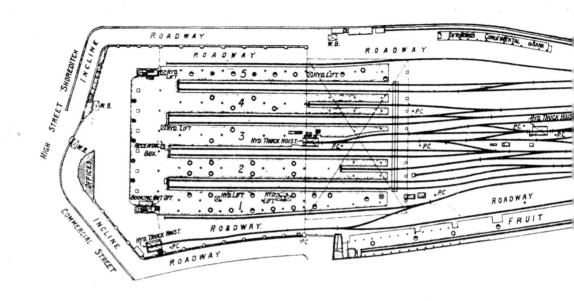

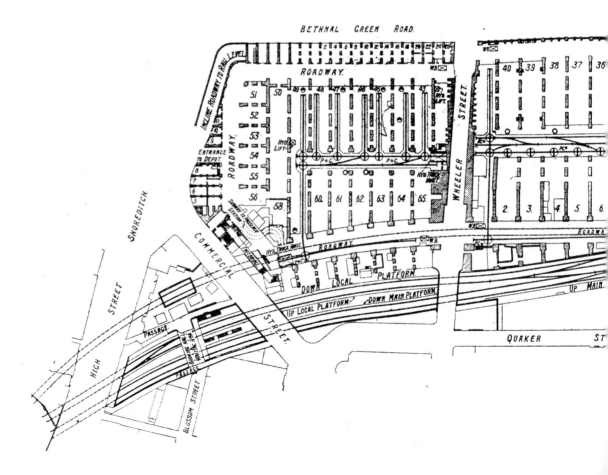

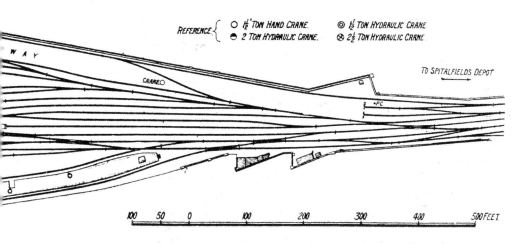

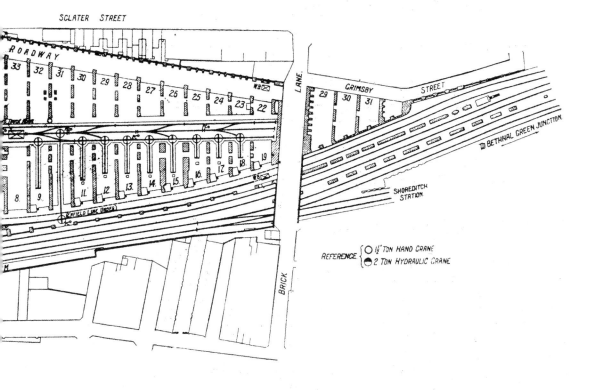

Historical plan of upper and lower rail levels showing the rails one story above grade and then the spaces under the supporting arches below. These spaces served as storage and as a marketplace for the goods arriving above.

SITE DEMOGRAPHICS BY LOCAL DISTRICT

LONDON'S BOROUGHS

TOWER HAMLETS 1
DENSITY: 415 PERSONS/HECTARE
RELIGION: 70% MUSLIM
EMPLOYED FULL TIME: 27%
ETHNICITY: 69% BANGLADESHI
AGE: 39% 1–17
     39% 18–49
     22% 40+

TOWER HAMLETS 2
DENSITY: 57 PERSONS/HECTARE
RELIGION: 37% MUSLIM
EMPLOYED FULL TIME: 50%
ETHNICITY: 42% WHITE, BRITISH
          34% BANGLADESHI
AGE: 21% 1–17
     53% 18–49
     26% 40+

SITE

HACKNEY
DENSITY: 30 PERSONS/HECTARE
RELIGION: 44% CHRISTIAN
EMPLOYED FULL TIME: 55%
ETHNICITY: 56% WHITE, BRITISH
AGE: 12% 1–17
     66% 18–49
     22% 40+

TOWER HAMLETS 3
DENSITY: 139 PERSONS/HECTARE
RELIGION: 64% MUSLIM
EMPLOYED FULL TIME: 31%
ETHNICIT Y: 63% BANGLADESHI
AGE: 31% 1–17
     41% 18–49
     28% 40+

CITY OF LONDON
DENSITY: 7 PERSONS/HECTARE
RELIGION: 57% CHRISTIAN
EMPLOYED FULL TIME: 73%
ETHNICITY: 67% WHITE, BRITISH
AGE: 6% 1–17
     59% 18–49
     35% 40+

TOWER HAMLETS 4
DENSITY: 73 PERSONS/HECTARE
RELIGION: 32% MUSLIM
EMPLOYED FULL TIME: 57%
ETHNICITY: 32% WHITE, BRITISH
          30% BANGLADESHI
AGE: 16% 1–17
     60% 18–49
     24% 40+

Bishopsgate Goods Yard in Greater London: D'Arcy Fenton Excerpts from a discussion with the studio about the project site.

The firm Hammerson has been creating office space for the London real estate market for more than a generation, redeveloping sites with new buildings better suited to the contemporary requirements of financial and legal occupants. Bishopsgate Goods Yard, because of its history, scale, and location on the edge of the City of London, and derelict condition, is a more complex proposition. While the City will require large-scale employment use, there is an imperative to develop a master plan with a mix of uses and urban spaces that will stitch back together a significant portion of London.

Around the site are many neighborhoods and constituencies. To the south and southwest is Broadgate, which has a series of developments that were started in the mid-1980s as way for the city to house the large financial and legal institutions that make London what it is. By staying out of the European monetary unit, London and Great Britain have positioned themselves extremely well to be brokers for the world. The demand for bespoke development has been ongoing—until the recession—creating new office buildings and housing in and around the city for the people who work there. The new development will be supported by the long increase in housing prices. The other constituencies include Spitalfields, a renewed neighborhood with a fine-grain street structure that was developed in the seventeenth century, and the Curtain Road area, which is still partially fractured but is being rejuvenated with new houses and creative industries such as architecture, graphic design, and cuisine. To the northwest is Shoreditch, an up-and-coming area. In the east, the Columbia Road and Bawdry Lane area is a conserved, established planned estate, and Bethnal Green Road leads to the East End and the Whitehall area, which is mainly characterized by a large, open space called Allan Gardens. To the south is Banglatown, or Brick Lane, which is the old, established market.

One can understand the challenge of fitting all these constituencies back together: the bankers, lawyers, and executives that work in the City, the market traders in Banglatown, and everyone else in-between. The site is in the midst of this mix, and Bishopsgate Goods Yard cuts off the south from the north and the east from the west. The area to the south is largely regenerated; Bishopsgate Goods Yard and the area to the north have been isolated from this phenomenon until now.

Because this area has been the focus of planners' hopes for years, many people are interested in the future of the site. For example, the so-called City Fringe group developed policies about how Bishopsgate Goods Yard could solve social and cultural problems as well as reintegrate the physical urban fabric. The Greater London Assembly (GLA), run by former Mayor Ken Livingston, is another force of development interests.

These vocal constituencies take the usual approach, wanting all the benefits of development but none of its drawbacks. On top of it all, many old and new rail lines run across the site, including the new East London Line. The Braithwaite vaults, named after the engineer who built the railhead in the 1840s, are the historically designated section of the original goods yard; the lines were about six meters above grade, so that when the trains would come in, they would be unloaded and the goods dropped into the vaults below for storage and distribution. Six meters below ground is a viaduct that contains the contemporary rail lines, which all terminate at Liverpool Street. Thus, in developing the area, we must keep the vaults and the rail lines, building around and over them. Thus, about thirty-two percent of the site remains for development.

Another pressure that will bear on this site is the London View Management Framework. In about 1950, London started to develop what it thought were the important views of St. Paul's, an architectural set piece for London and the most important building in Britain. Taller development threatened the views of the dome and lantern of St. Paul's against the skyline, and we had to take that under consideration by not designing new buildings within those view corridors. The buildings have to be shaped to take the views into account.

The design will be developed with the relevant public bodies. They have formed a forum, comprising the Greater London Authority, the Boroughs of Hackney and Tower Hamlets, and Transport for London. The scheme will move forward through a dialogue of proposals and feedback, thus knitting together public and private needs.

In terms of connections, we are looking around the site and what Bishopsgate Goods Yard can actually influence, because regeneration should extend to the context surrounding the site. The master plan first seeks to repair the street network, reconnect it through the site, and then encourage the sort of movement needed to develop urban areas. In doing that we hope to engage the huge flows of people coming out of Liverpool Street into Spitalfields Market and Bishops Square along Brushfield Street, up Commercial Street, up Shoreditch High Street, then across our site to connect to Brick Lane and to Allen Gardens to the east. We are going to develop routes through the existing arch structure and the new East London Line viaduct, with public uses on the internal street frontages as well as on Slater Street and Bethnal Green Road.

We will create plots for office spaces, residential spaces, retail, and public uses to meet the objectives for employment and living. We want as many uses as possible to replicate those that create lively cities. Both the public space and commercial space must engage uses and demand for the overall master plan to succeed.

The master plan must create a lively integration of all the objectives as well as the public and private spaces that make a city thrive, tapping into the energy of the surrounding areas. The master plan must have a phasing strategy that allows the development to quickly start to finance itself, while establishing the key public spaces that will create the desirability that can attract investment. The master plan must deliver all these things to become viable.

A panorama of Shoreditch's High Street.

Architectures of the City, Separated by a Common Language: John McMorrough The city, as a scale of design, manifests a series of assumptions and limitations. These circumstances include not only questions of how to address the city's problems (what goes where, in what quantities, in which direction, and for how long), but also issues of how to respond to its problematics (that is, how design can be implemented at such a scale, and what claims of agency and authorship this implies). As architecture imagines itself at a larger scale, namely, that of the city, it must acknowledge that the city is concerned with a multiplicity mostly beyond architecture's more singularly focused comfort zone. The city itself is inherently multiple, and while there are architectures of multiplicity, architects don't design whole cities (for lots of reasons). But many architects still envision whole cities (or large portions thereof) as a project type, whether out of necessity or of their own volition, and these projects give an understanding of how cities and architecture operate as a conceptual challenge. Over the last sixty years, architecture has had to confront the challenges of city-making, and whether through historical reference, scale, or programmatic accumulation, the attempts have tended toward a re-creation of long-term temporal effects in a relatively brief period of time. The production of the Nick Johnson / FAT Yale studio enacts not only the general problematics of architectural engagement with the city over the last sixty years—issues of definition, control, agency, and vision—but, in consolidating these issues, uncovers the particular question of how architecture in this relative immediacy can invoke the temporal accumulations associated with the city.

So, given that architecture's general ambition is to re-create the effects of time (achieved by means of definition, control, agency, and vision) within contemporary urbanism, consideration of the city's future presents a terrain of continual redefinition, initiated with new information, contexts, and contingencies. Out of these new pressures a reaction takes place—new connections are made and alternatives envisioned. The proposal to design the city is best understood neither as a set of operations and techniques nor as specific scales and densities, but as the articulation of the very possibility of propositions: a model of design in and of the world. A city can be defined by its population, economics, or infrastructure, and while architects have increasingly availed themselves of these considerations, architecture primarily defines the city by its formal and physical implications. In terms of urban agglomeration, by definition, when there is no formal or physical implication, these are no longer the concerns of the architect; they become an issue of planning.

Of the scales of design, the connection of urban design to the world seems the most direct, while its means seem the most removed. The connectedness is reflected in the fact that city design proposes to organize the variety of systems (infrastructural, logistical, ecological, and social) comprising the modern city. The making of a city, however, is not a singular act; it entails a series of multiple contingencies and constituencies. Urban design cannot simply assume authority (it is not empowered by fiat), but rather must construct it from a situation of only-always partial information and empowerment. Such remoteness ensures it operates by way of plans, schemes, and maneuvers: mediated expressions of mediated desires. In this sense the design of the city constitutes above all a form of consensus-building—its expertise is to communicate and convince. The success of urbanism is measured not just in its capacity to describe and propose, but its ability to instill confidence and enable the extended body politic to mobilize and enact even the most minimal of propositions. If the city is defined by a formal presence, the available means to control the city are frequently thwarted by the city's multitudinous forces. The implicit substratum for a desire to define is a desire to control, and if the promise of control is the aspiration of the architect, the site of the city is its largest manifestation and frustration.

With the city's multiple constituencies, the formulation of definition and control happens within a con-stellation of urban decision-makers, and agency grows out of control. For the planner, agency results from a consolidation of difference—among constituencies, agencies, and so on—to create a consensus, but the desired specificity of architecture, in terms of definition and control, is poorly served by such democratic models. The planning professions, as formless orchestrations of logistics, find their embodi-ment in the relentless regularity and most restrictive implementation of "new" Urbanism. Architecture, as a more formally progressive version of urban definition (in that it seeks to make the new rather than repeat formulae), operates without a sense of legislation and thus depends on a system of realization that can only enact the status quo (the differences among the mall, the megastructure, the park, and the parking lot become negligible in the sense of implementation). If architecture hopes to create something beyond the compromises of consensus, it needs to exhibit another form of agency, even if the form of this agency is infrequently called upon.

The nature of that particular form of architectural agency for the city is, simply, vision—the imagining of the city yet to be. Over the past sixty or so years, architecture has attempted to work its way around the issues of consensual urbanism or urbanism left solely to the vagaries of time. A vision unites these heterogeneous forces. But the baggage brought with the vision is both historical (in terms

of expressionism and authorial impositions) and contemporary (the corporate notion of "added value"), prompting a redemption of vision from these associations so that the city may be positioned as more than personal (in its evocation of the collective) and more than mercantile (which it must, nonetheless, engage). Neither the authoritarianism of grand schemes nor the abstinence of incremental urbanism seems adequate to the task—they assume either too much or too little. So the means of such urban design must navigate the poles of impotence and omnipotence, falling somewhere in between—idealistic enough to propose the new but contingent enough to suspect the limits of its authority. This approach has not been an issue of style or period or some kind of artistic cultural grouping but can be read in projects as diverse as Team X and New Urbanism, which situate the architects' description of the city in relation to their agency and control, under the aegis of vision. The typical (block sizes, zoning regulations, building codes), the exceptional (attractions, amenities, indigenous features), the quantitative (lengths, heights, populations, demographics), and the qualitative (ambience, image, identity) are multiplicities for which envisioning their correspondence requires description and discrimination.

The condition to which each iteration of architects makes tacit reference is the necessarily timely component of the urban composition versus the relative immediacy and finality of architectural form, emergence versus delineation or proscription versus prescription. The question of how to marshal the heterogeneity of urban forces into the homogeneity of a singular design act remains. In the contemporary sense, the urban question has been concerned with the subject of networks in the evocation of the parametric or the emergence of the issues described, which, one could argue, has been the fulfillment of the same desire as the collage city, to have within its operative logic the possibility of description, contrasts, continuities, and distinctions. Though stylistically different, they are, within the conceptual topography of urbanism, the same designers of the same problematic.

In looking at the work of the studio, one is, of course, aware of FAT's engagement with the detritus of architectural Post-Modernism, of interest not as descendents of a lineage but rather as self-described inheritors of a constructed history. Each project, in addition to operating as a stratagem in the studio, also reflects the current possibility for the architectural imagination of the city: a green-roof strategy; a megastructure (and mat building) as collage; the use of scale, superposition, and rotation of legible (read "gabled") architectural form; the dense packing of autarkic towers; and the use of ruination and fragmentation (aka indexicality), to name a few. Relatively speaking, the projects are the historic and archaic, the anarchistic, the market-based, and the non sequitur. What is retained is not the inevitability of architectural form but architectural mass—the need to describe the results of the design process in terms of discretely imaginable results. It is here that the effort of the Johnson / FAT studio is relevant to the question of such matters: the surrounding collage-like appearance of many of the schemes is only a particular manifestation of the general impetus (within the studio and within the field) to understand the strictly architectural capacity of massing to inform and produce an urban image.

The extensive, seemingly protean uncontrollability of the city is counter to architecture's ambitions of control. The site of the city, as a limit case for the possibility of control, has been a continual reference within the architectural imagination, especially as to what extent it is possible to read the will of one in the aspirations of another. It is the promise of urban design to address the problems of the city, and its value resides not solely in its answers but also in its questions. Even though in the game of making the city architects are dealt a losing hand (at a remove from the positions of power that in the end decide the fate of the city), investigations like those of this studio make important contributions in the conceptual-ization of possibility in which the city eventually takes shape. The contemporary status of urbanism is not only a practice but also a mode of investigation.

The outer roadside of the original arched wall on the northern perimeter of the site is to be retained.

III. BISHOPS GOODS YARD STUDIO WO

Bishopsgate Goods Yard Studio Brief: FAT The Bishopsgate Goods Yard studio, led by the team of FAT architects and Nick Johnson, began with a critique of the assumed neutrality of contemporary master-planning. Developer-led revitalization has a particular way of looking at the world; its intentions are directed by complex financial instruments manifested through an architectural brief allied to a totalizing urban vision.

These singular concerns were reflected in a master plan for the site designed by Foster + Partners for the London-based developer Hammersons. This proposal follows in the tradition of other recent brownfield-regenerated business districts such as Docklands, Broadgate, and Paddington Basin, in London. These schemes present a particular form of urban design as normative, benign, and as an inevitable progression of urban landscape from industrial to postindustrial. These schemes deliver "mixed use" in a singularly homogeneous manner, the kind of "difference" symptomatic of advanced capitalism.

The studio proposed a more radically expanded idea of mixed use for Bishopsgate in which cultural differences generate a complex set of relationships acted out through urban design. In this approach, social and cultural issues confront aesthetics. Symbolic language, meaning, and communication become devices that articulate the social and cultural agendas of different populations, making difference explicit.

Bishopsgate Goods Yard is situated at the intersection of several different Londons: London's financial district, the fashionista playground of Shoreditch, the Bangladeshi community of Brick Lane, and the East End of Whitechapel. Dealing-room floors, curry houses, merchant banks, artfully dishevelled bars, flea markets, coffee shops, designer furniture dealers, art galleries, expensive restaurants, warehouses, sari shops, and all-night bagel bakeries coexist within a few hundred yards of each other.

Perhaps the inevitable fate of the goods yard is to become the point of intersection of these competing interests, a place where typologies, tastes, the designed, and the found are juxtaposed in ways that suggest both unresolvable conflict and synergystic brotherhood. Social housing and trading floors form alliances, and kebab shops intersect with high-end restaurants. New hybrid architectural languages are precipitated by unlikley solutions.

In this way, revitalization and master-planning become a highly specific and engaged activity, generating architectural scenarios that demand shrewd tactics combined with wide-eyed innocence to examine relationships among spatial arrangements, historical precedent, architectural typology, and proposed populations.

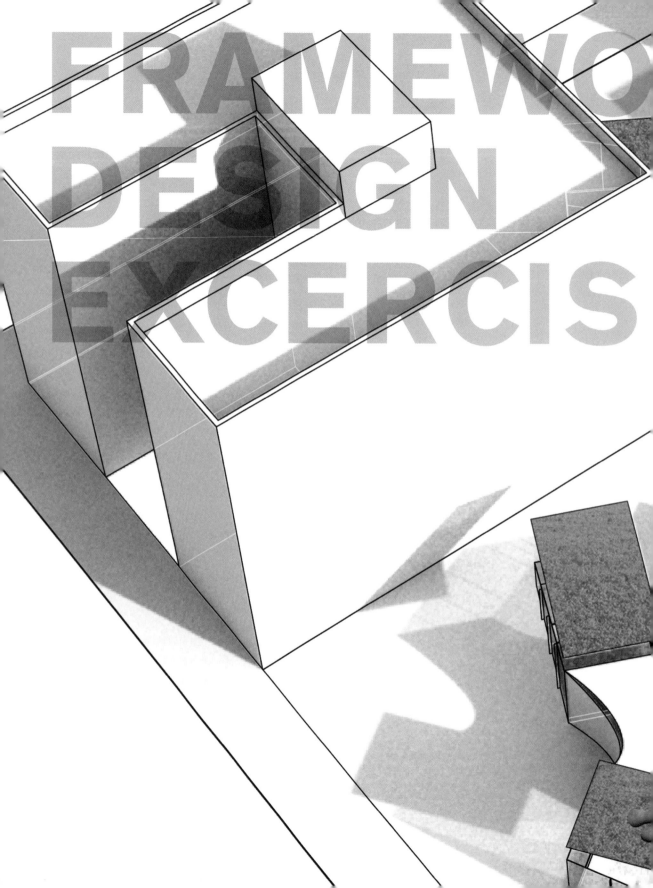

The studio began with a series of design exercises that addressed programmatic recombination, hybrid-izing architectural language, and investigating ways of representing the occupation of space. These gestures acted as explorations of particular architectural ideas and tactics to develop an armory and vocabulary for the studio.

The studio was asked to record in forensic detail the minutiae of relationships between objects and people—situations such as the line for a late-night kebab or the politics of disco dancing. At this detailed level, very specific relationships among use, spatial organization, and objects were revealed. By recog-nizing the specificity of everyday situations as equally viable sites for architectural concern, the studio proposed an alternative to the generic idea of spatial meaning in normative master-planning.

Reaching back through the history of architecture, the studio exhumed architectural styles that were then recomposed into new hybrids. Here, techniques of the avant-garde—juxtaposition, montage, collage—were applied to the ideas of nineteenth-century architectural historian Bannister Fletcher. Through the manipulations of diverse langauges, the studio developed an attitude toward the way in which architectural language communicates.

Looking at ways of combining diverse programs paired synergistic pragmatism with cultural attitude. In contrast to most contemporary developments, these hybrids suggested ways of forming engaged relationships among traditionally distinct activities and demonstrated the potential of programs to act as social condensers, which might activate relationships among the diverse conditions neighboring Bishopsgate Goods Yard.

x100 If you repeat a word one hundred times, the word begins to lose its meaning. It starts to sound strange, and its cognitive aspect dissolves. The more you say it, the more alien it seems to become. Suddenly, language, which usually flows naturally from our mouths, feels unnatural—as though it were a newly invented gadget. Which, relatively speaking, it is.

At the beginning of the semester the students were asked to apply this concept to a design exercise as a fast and furious riff resulting in one hundred drawings. The students were to choose a building or an everyday object, whether a generic product of a rational and unspectacular kind of international modernism or a product of corporate or mass-produced ordinariness. The one hundred drawings were prompted by questions of how a person or identity might alter the design, how a condition or state might modify it, or how un-architectural attributes might provide meaning.

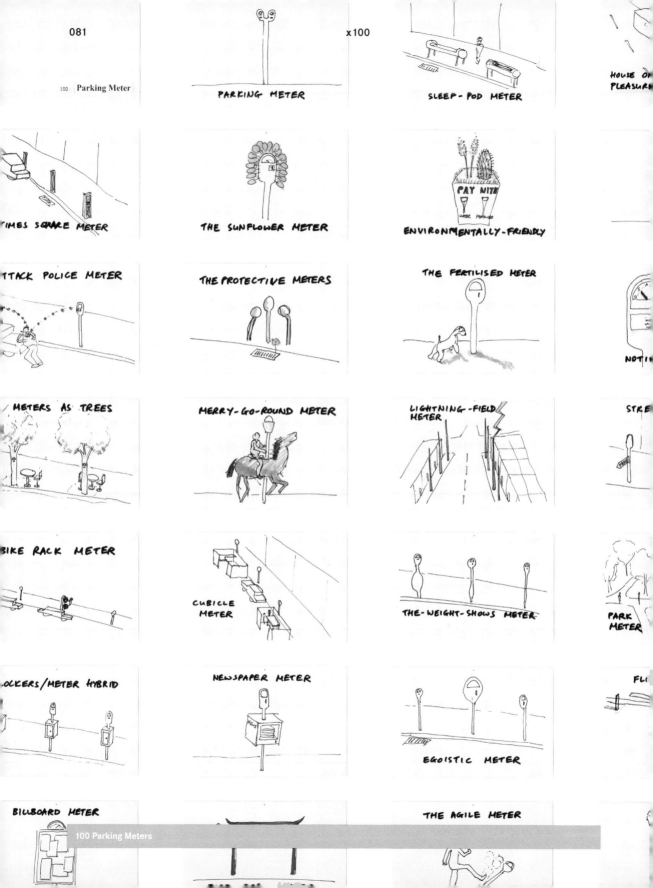

x100

100 Parking Meter

PARKING METER

SLEEP - POD METER

HOUSE OF
PLEASURE

TIMES SQUARE METER

THE SUNFLOWER METER

ENVIRONMENTALLY-FRIENDLY

PAY WITH

TTACK POLICE METER

THE PROTECTIVE METERS

THE FERTILISED METER

NOTI

METERS AS TREES

MERRY-GO-ROUND METER

LIGHTNING-FIELD
METER

STRE

BIKE RACK METER

CUBICLE
METER

THE-WEIGHT-SHOWS METER

PARK
METER

OCKERS/METER HYBRID

NEWSPAPER METER

EGOISTIC METER

FL

BILLBOARD METER

THE AGILE METER

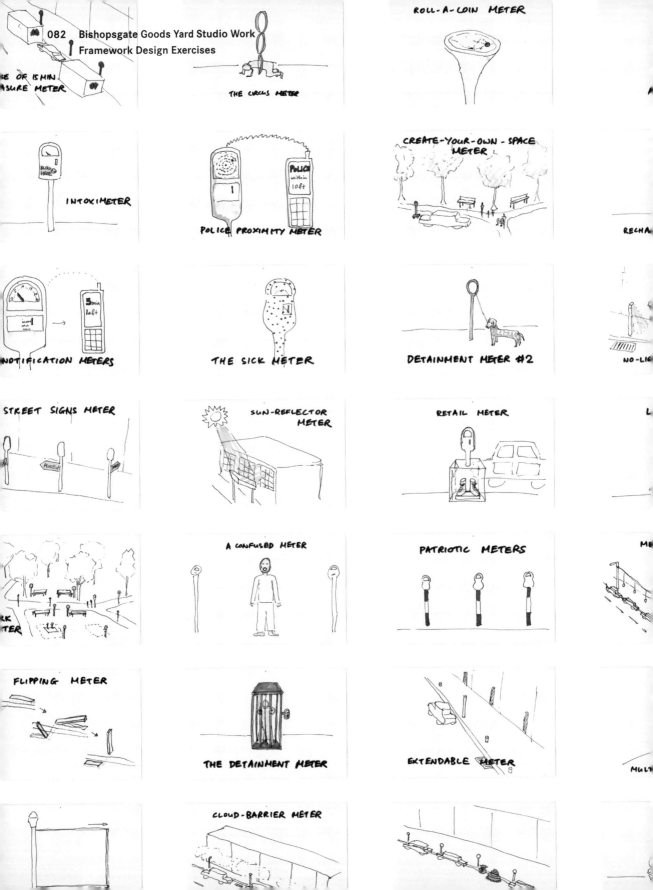

USE OF 15 MIN
MEASURE METER

THE CIRCUS METER

ROLL-A-COIN METER

INTOXIMETER

POLICE PROXIMITY METER

CREATE-YOUR-OWN-SPACE
METER

RECHA

NOTIFICATION METERS

THE SICK METER

DETAINMENT METER #2

NO-LIG

STREET SIGNS METER

SUN-REFLECTOR
METER

RETAIL METER

L

RK
TER

A CONFUSED METER

PATRIOTIC METERS

ME

FLIPPING METER

THE DETAINMENT METER

EXTENDABLE METER

MULT

CLOUD-BARRIER METER

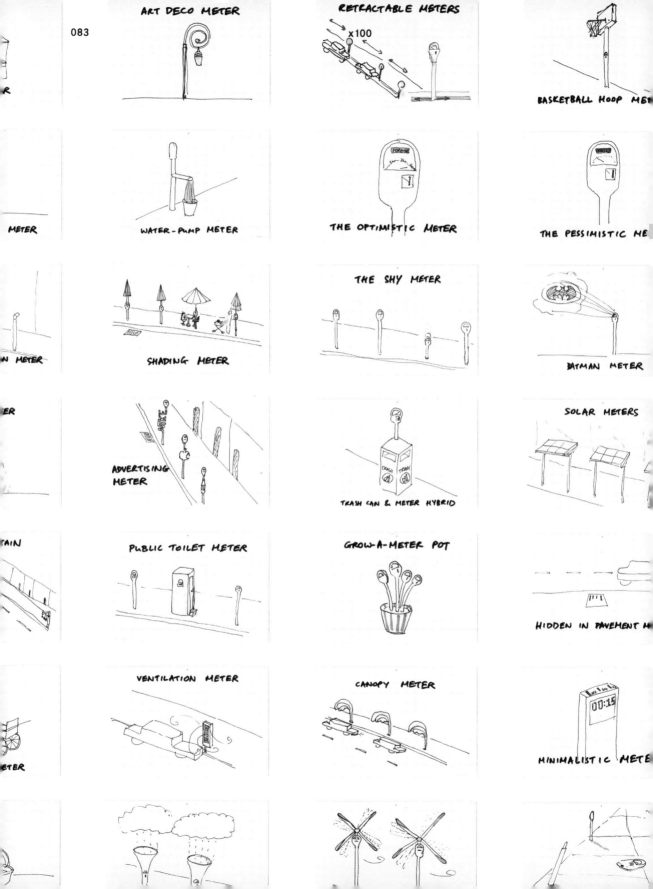

083

ART DECO METER

RETRACTABLE METERS

x100

BASKETBALL HOOP METER

METER

WATER-PUMP METER

THE OPTIMISTIC METER

THE PESSIMISTIC METER

N METER

SHADING METER

THE SHY METER

BATMAN METER

ER

ADVERTISING METER

TRASH CAN & METER HYBRID

SOLAR METERS

TAIN

PUBLIC TOILET METER

GROW-A-METER POT

HIDDEN IN PAVEMENT METER

TER

VENTILATION METER

CANOPY METER

MINIMALISTIC METER

People in Architecture Architectural drawings are normally used to depict walls and objects rather than people or experiences. But architecture is inhabited. It both shapes and is shaped by the activities and people it houses. It organizes bodies in space by means of how the spaces are arranged. It also organizes people's behavior through the use of signs and symbols. Being in a cheap diner is different from being in a classy restaurant, even if they are the same size and shape. Similarly, to be in Times Square as a tourist is different than being there as a policeman.

This assignment asked the students to use drawings to describe not just what is there, but who is there: who "they" are, and what they are doing. The students were to describe visually what kind of place it is. Is it easy to get to? Do you have to pay? Do you need to be a member? Is it grand and imposing or intimate and friendly? Is it the site of a horror film or a romantic comedy? The students had to investigate in detail what it is like: is it dark or light, clean or dirty? Is there a cracked window or a broken toilet? What is the sofa like? Is there a stain on the carpet? Is it hot, cold, damp, or on fire?

Further, they had to pay close attention to the sequence and organization of the spaces. Are they open or closed in character? Are there changes in level or ceiling height?

They were asked to choose three very different spaces, which could be similar in function but different in scale—for example, the entrance to your house, the entrance to a bar, and the entrance to the U.N. building. Or they might be similar in scale but very different in function—a bedroom, a boardroom, and a doctor's waiting room. The students then drew each space to communicate the differences. The drawings were to be precise and analytical, rather than blandly atmospheric or expressionistic, and illustrate people as well as condition, time of day, or any other salient evidence in terms of who uses the space and how.

CRIME SCENE: 28 HIGH ST. APARTMENT 8, NEW HAVEN, CT, SEPTEMBER 17, 2007

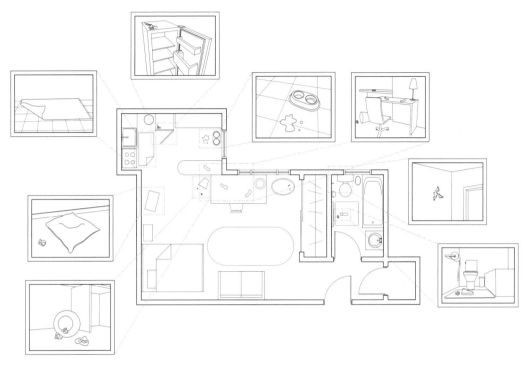

EVIDENCE GATHERED AT THE SCENE OF THE CRIME

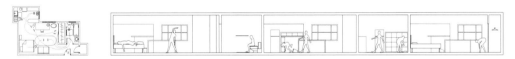

SUSPECT #1: CHRISTINA WU, TIME INSIDE APARTMENT: 8:30PM-9:15AM, 10:57AM-11:00AM

SUSPECT #2: BERNIE THE DOG, TIME INSIDE APARTMENT: 8:30PM-11:00AM

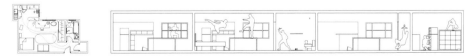

SUSPECT #3: THE NINJA, TIME INSIDE APARTMENT: 11:10AM-11:45AM

Without relying on the typical architectural convention of walls and floors, this drawing depicts a crime scene involving three suspects. The remnants they left behind in their occupation of the space becomes evidence to solve the crime.

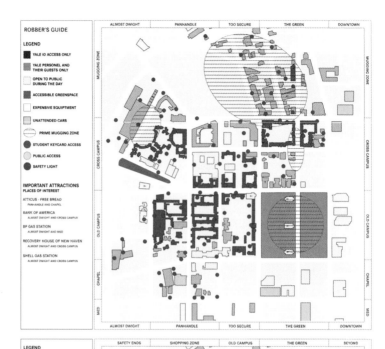

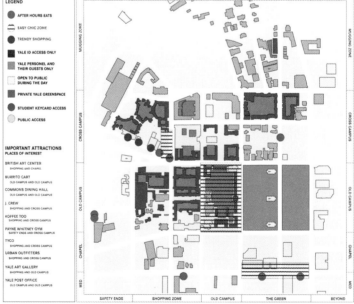

(Above) The Yale Campus Pop-Out Map shows how a single place can be mapped and coded for different user groups. The top map provides information that would be useful to a robber on campus, while the bottom maps the campus according to the interests of a Yale undergraduate student. (Opposite) The stories of three banal events are told using pictograms to signify actions. These new icons illustrate the activities of going to the bank, using the subway, and going to a coffee shop.

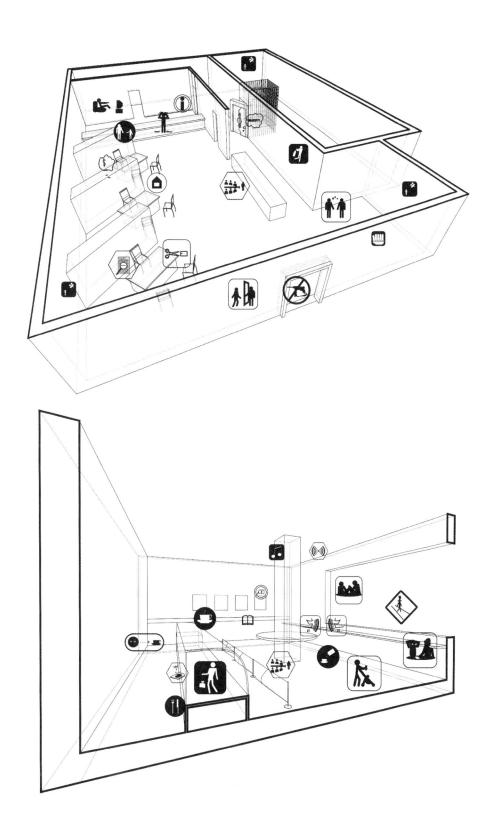

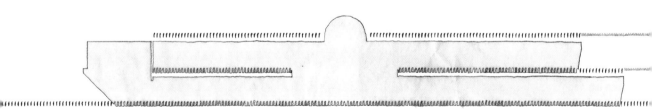

The scale of people in relationship to space can vary greatly from building to building. Sections of two of the most important religious places in the world, Mecca, in Saudi Arabia and St. Peter's Cathedral, in Italy, explain the grandeur of each place by comparing the buildings' interior space and the scale of the people within it.

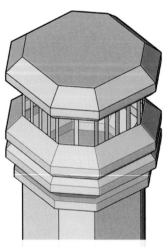

3 into 1 In another exercise, the students were asked to explore a design for combinations of uses, users, contexts, and languages.

They were asked to design a place, a space, or a building that could serve three very different constituencies with different sets of criteria. These criteria were derived from categories such as individual, communal, institutional, ceremonial, informal, domestic, official, and unplanned. The types of users would be just as diverse.

Students addressed the relevant languages of different uses. The challenge was to not dislocate function from its cultural context. Students were asked to make reference to appropriate materials, decorative elements, furniture, and ancillary objects.

Some suggestions provided were "operating theater, opera, and Oprah," as well as "soccer field, meeting room, and library."

This exercise became illustrated in axonometric drawings with annotations—labels, details, and references—to help build up the scenario. Each student was to use a different kind of tactic—such as juxtaposition, overlaying, merging, or doublings and triplings—folded into the same place.

HeadBANGers, BANGers and mash, and BANGladeshi are combined here by colliding the forms and decoration of the CBGB club in New York, the Equestrian Pub in England, and a traditional mosque.

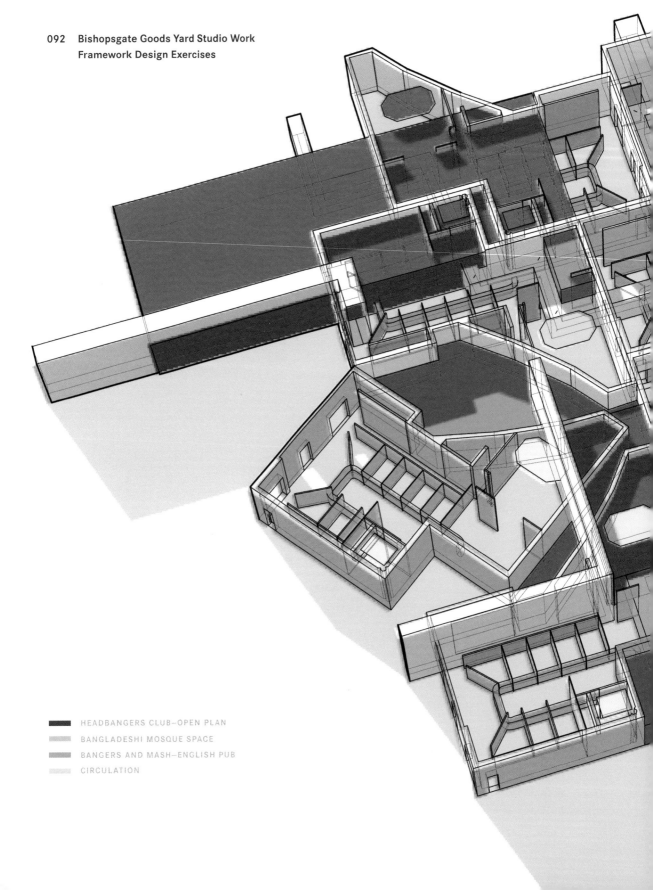

HEADBANGERS CLUB—OPEN PLAN
BANGLADESHI MOSQUE SPACE
BANGERS AND MASH—ENGLISH PUB
CIRCULATION

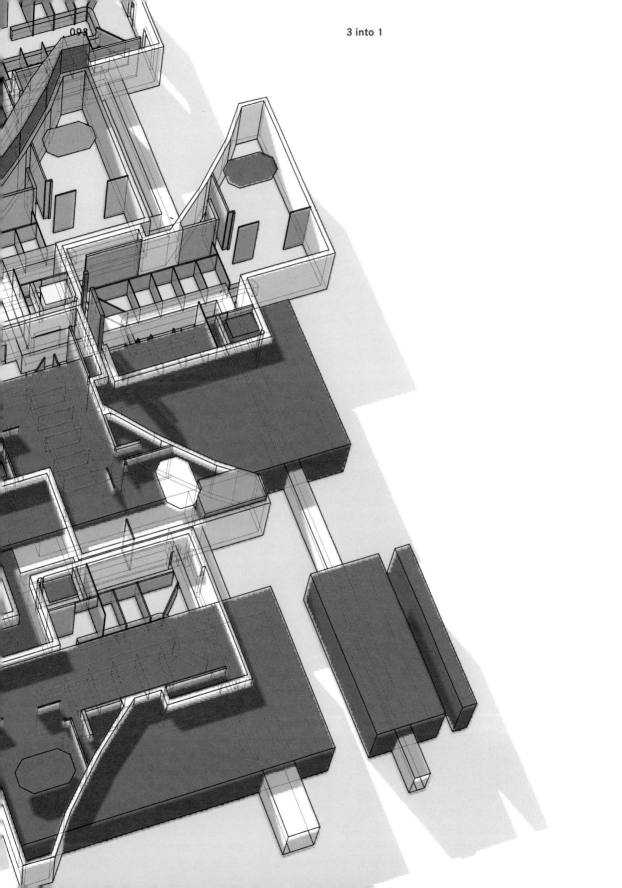

1A OUTDOOR GARDEN
1B GREENHOUSE GARDEN
2   COURTS (8)
3   MEETING ROOMS (4)

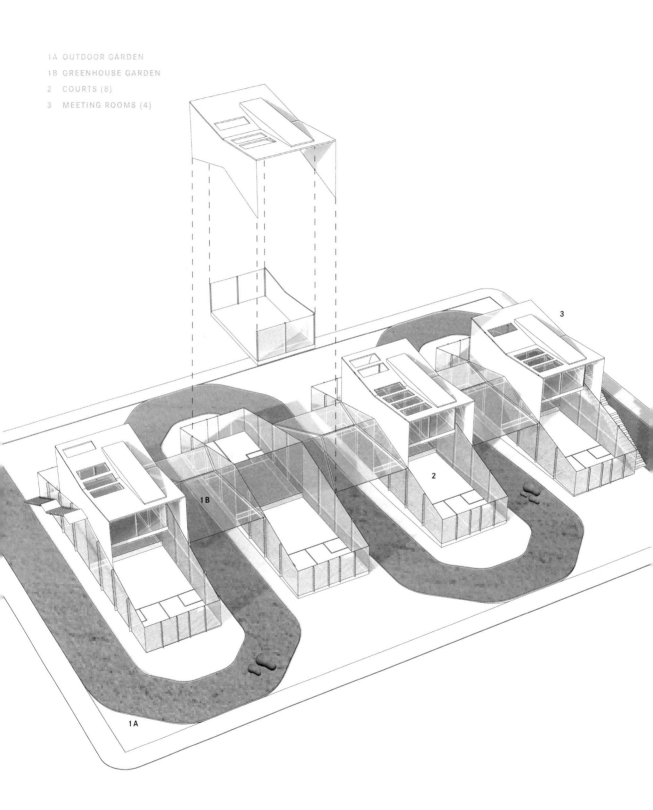

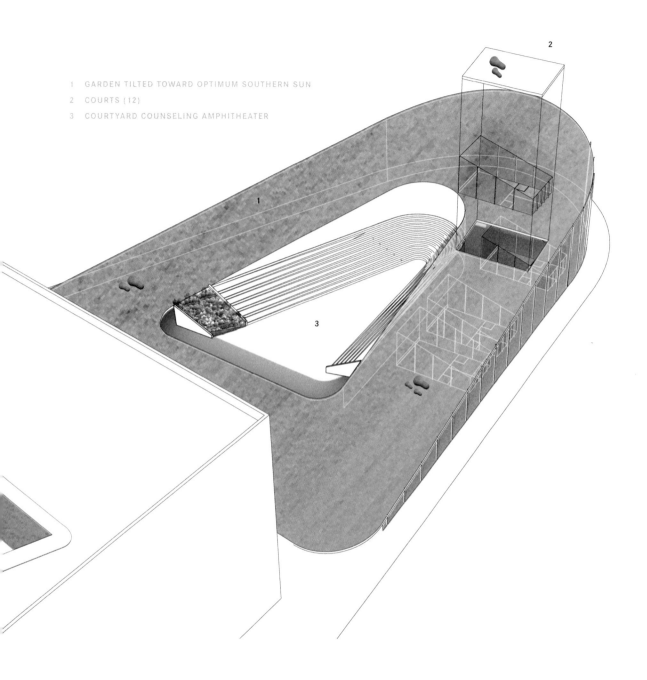

1   GARDEN TILTED TOWARD OPTIMUM SOUTHERN SUN

2   COURTS (12)

3   COURTYARD COUNSELING AMPHITHEATER

Community fitness, urban farming, and drug rehabilitation support groups are combined together and contextualized onto three different types of sites, a rectangular site, a triangular site, and an infill site, showing the adaptability of meshed programs.

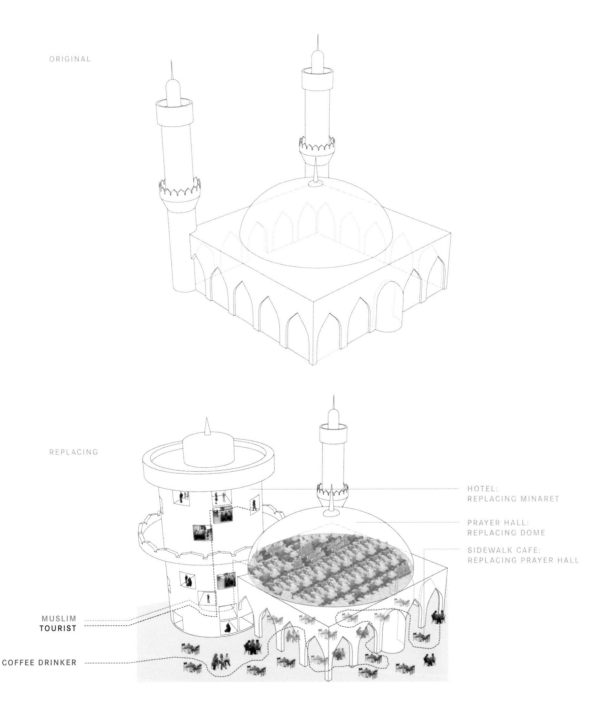

ORIGINAL

REPLACING

HOTEL:
REPLACING MINARET

PRAYER HALL:
REPLACING DOME

SIDEWALK CAFE:
REPLACING PRAYER HALL

MUSLIM
TOURIST

COFFEE DRINKER

Starting with a mosque typology, the programs of a hotel, a prayer hall, and a sidewalk café are merged into one building. Formally, the idea is realized through the techniques of replacing, nesting, and weaving of existing as well as invented architectural elements.

NESTING

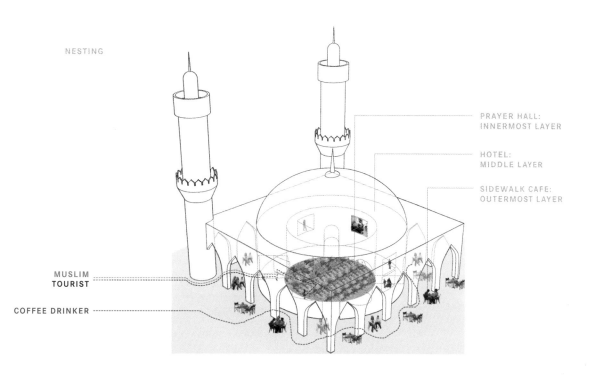

PRAYER HALL:
INNERMOST LAYER

HOTEL:
MIDDLE LAYER

SIDEWALK CAFE:
OUTERMOST LAYER

MUSLIM
TOURIST

COFFEE DRINKER

MEANDERING

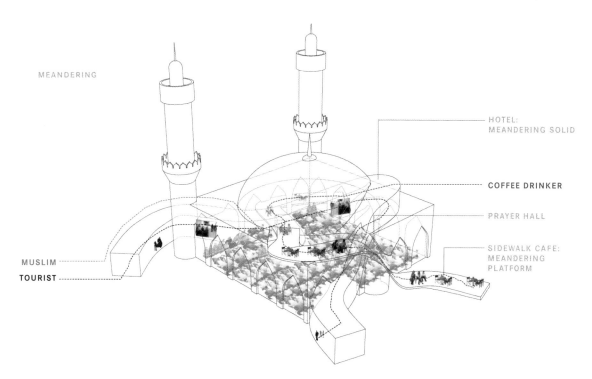

HOTEL:
MEANDERING SOLID

COFFEE DRINKER

PRAYER HALL

SIDEWALK CAFE:
MEANDERING
PLATFORM

MUSLIM
TOURIST

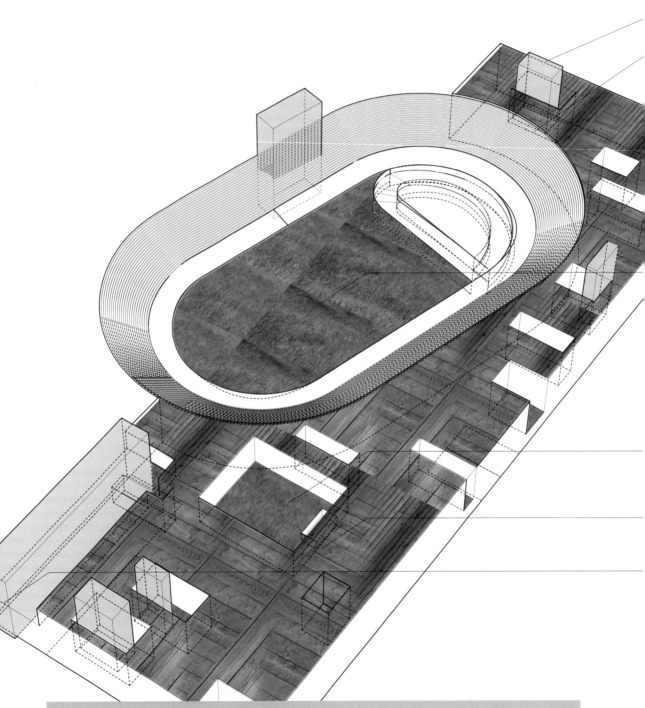

The development of a new building typology through the programmatic recombination of an elementary school, a velodrome, and an office block into a single structure organized around a series of shared courtyards and lightwells. With this configuration, the roof deck becomes the major point of interaction between the various users.

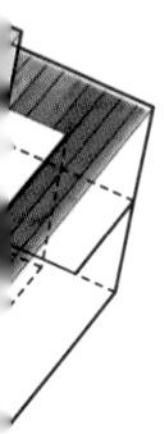

LIGHT WELLS

VELODROME SEATING

COMMUNAL COURTYARD

SUB-COURTYARD

ROOF DECK

SCHOOL ENTRANCE

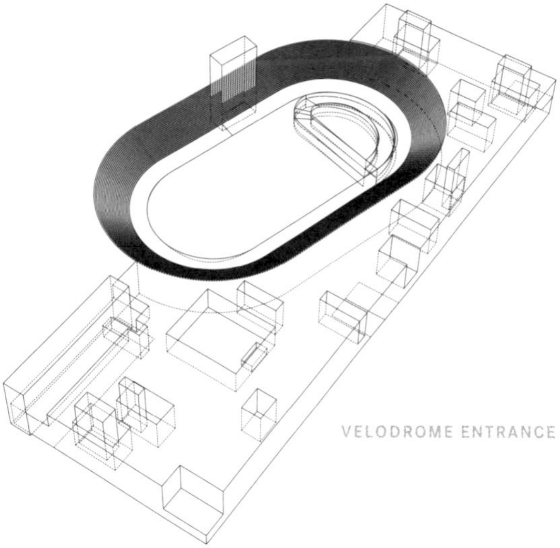

VELODROME ENTRANCE

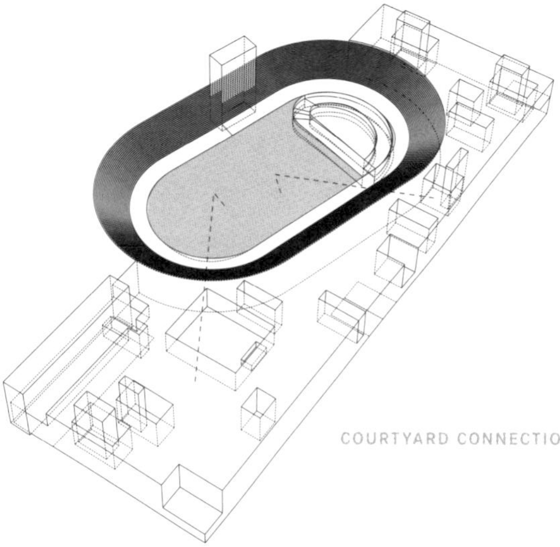

COURTYARD CONNECTIONS

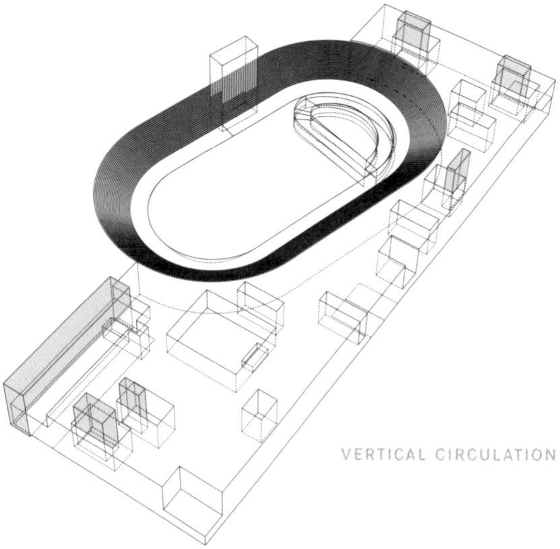

VERTICAL CIRCULATION

Bricolage The next exercise was to design three buildings in nine days using the design method bricolage, which creates an object, space, or environment through the collection and assembly of disparate elements. The elements could be invented, found, or manipulated in some way—through scale or some other form of distortion—and could have common, juxtaposed, or oppositional properties.

Copying is a means of doing architecture quickly. It stands in opposition to the drive for formal originality that characterizes much architectural production. However, the copying is not as easy as it seems, largely because the way one steals is as important as what one steals.

While the three buildings might or might not have a function or represent a given condition or mood, they each had to achieve differentiated qualities through either a violent (or not so violent) clash of architectural styles, a juxtaposition of scales and/or materials, an inversion of positive and negative elements, the "overcoding" of the composition with narrative elements, or a conflation of representational and/or abstract elements.

The students could steal ideas from existing buildings, well known or not, rescale them, crash them into other bits either stolen from elsewhere or invented in architectural styles of any period—Classical, Gothic, or Modern. They could even choose a building they hated as a starting point and then "clash" it into their favorite building.

They were asked to think about how the different elements relate to each other. Do they morph into, weave seamlessly around, awkwardly juxtapose against, or intersect each other? The students employed the techniques of repetition, superimposition, juxtaposition, rescaling, and recontextualization.

A country view from upstate New York overlaid with Indian urban figure-ground imagery—inspired by Constant Nieuwenhuys, industrial silhouettes and Michael Graves' perspectives—combines things both loved and hated into a single image.

This plan combines techniques employed by Kisho Kurakawa in his 1969 Capsule Tower with a module reminiscent of the Smithsons' House of the Future.

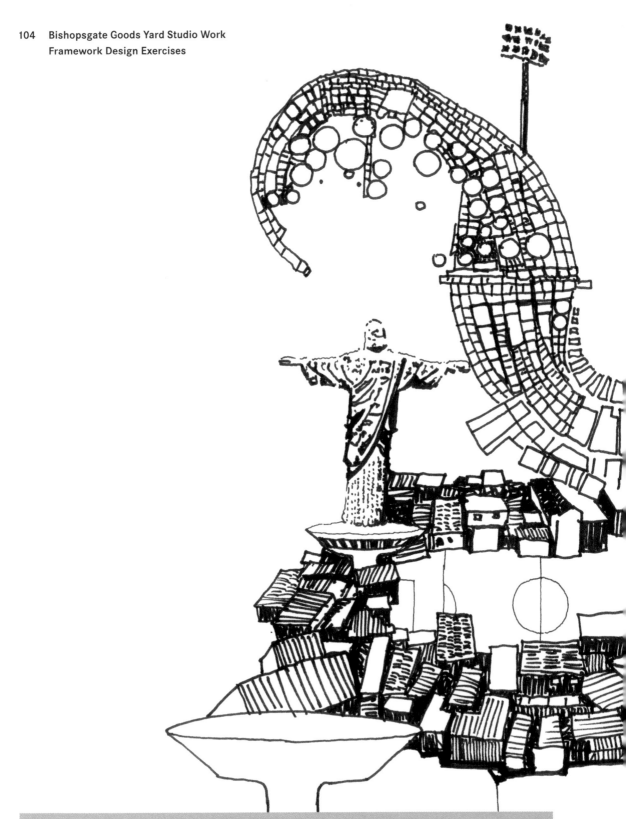

Brazilia imagines the integration of high and low culture by introducing the soccer stadium into the dense urban fabric of the *favelas*. The city/stadium suggests a more inclusive architecture, rich with demographic and stylistic overlaps.

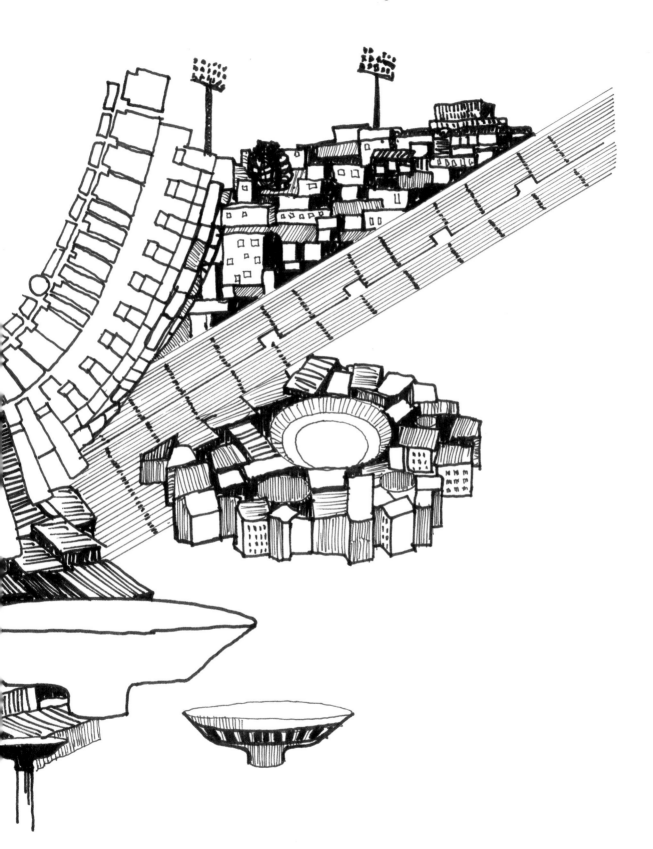

"River of Alternative Futures" combines a Frank Lloyd Wright fireplace and ceiling, a Yona Freidman drawing, and an El Lissitzky painting into a postapocalyptic urban rendering.

COLLAGE STUDIES

PLAN

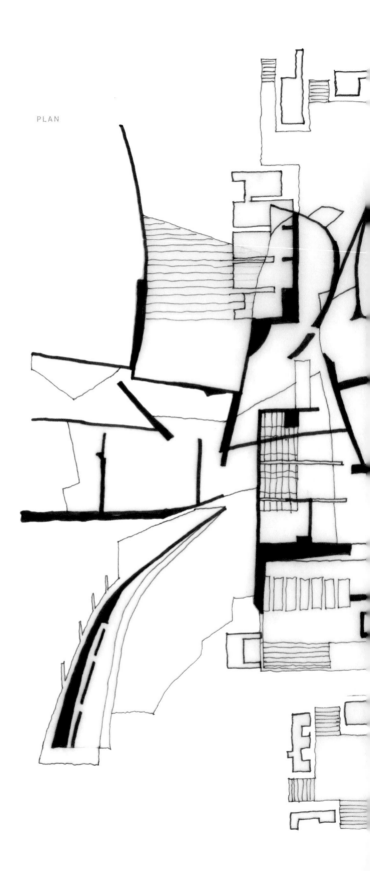

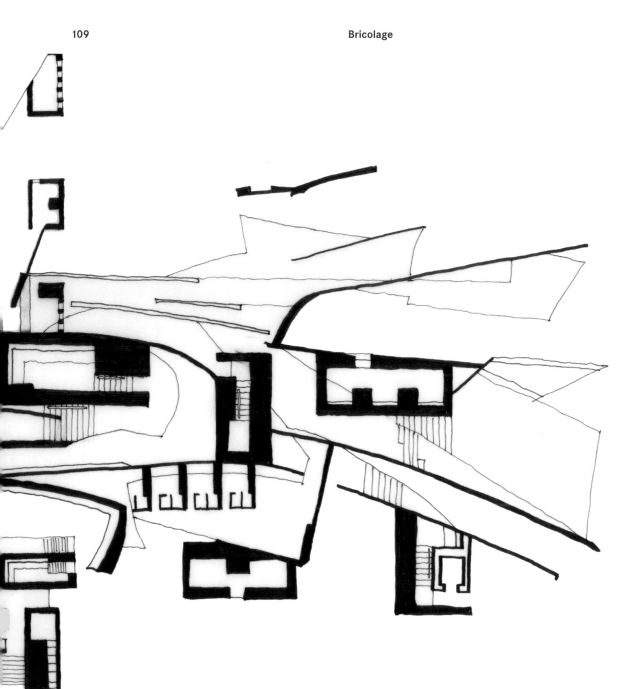

Examination of new spatial configurations created from the collaging of Peter Zumthor's Therme Vals and Frank Gehry's Bilbao Guggenheim Museum, while allowing the original plans to remain visible.

AXONOMETRIC

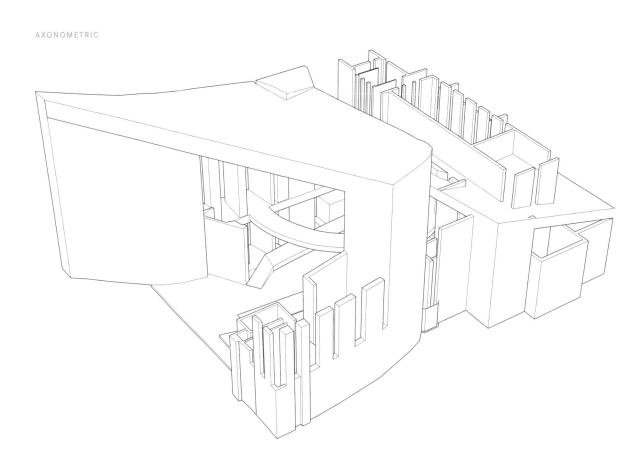

COLLAGE STUDIES

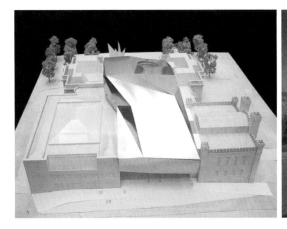

COLLAGE STUDIES

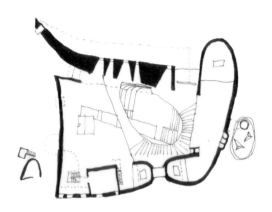

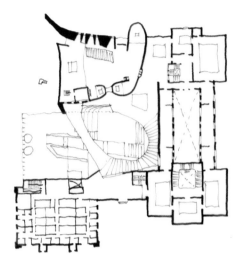

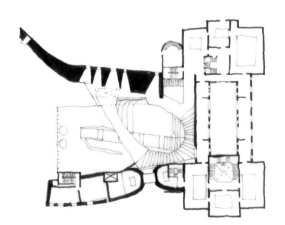

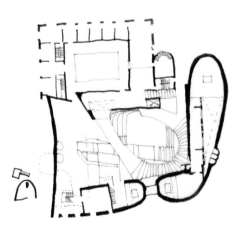

Studies of the combination of Le Corbusier's Ronchamp with the Wadsworth Atheneum Museum of Art by UNStudio, creating a form reminiscent of both while at the same time being completely new.

x100 Site Proposals Next, the students were asked to produce one hundred versions of their site proposals to address varieties of scale and content using techniques of sketching, collage, and paper cuts to communicate their ideas. They combined these sketches on index cards into a schematic version from an aerial viewpoint.

The program was derived from what existed and what was lacking in Bishopsgate, and used mixed-use and maxed-out scenarios such as cultural programs, housing, office space, and retail, with all their potentials.

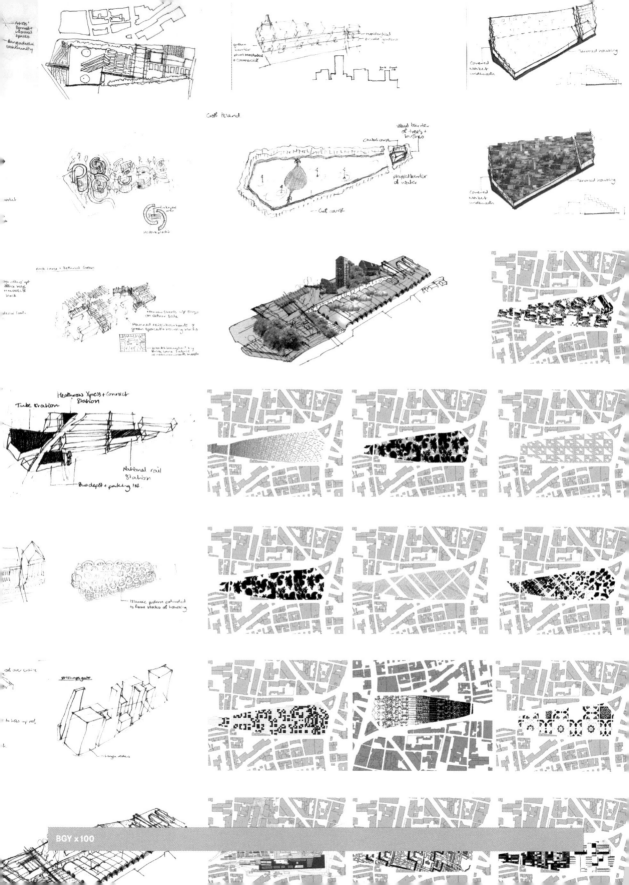

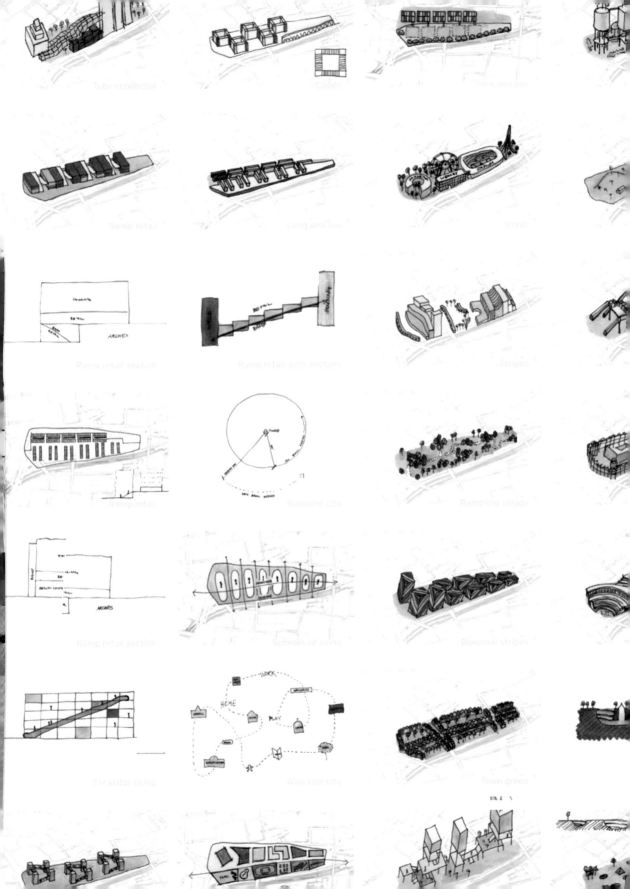

Tube connector

Cubes

Parkland ave

Ramp retail

Long and low

Iconic

Ramp retail section

Ramp retail with anchors

Stripes

Ramp retail

Walkable city

Rambling village

Ramp retail section

Spheres of living

Diagonal stripes

Escalator living

Walkable city

Town green

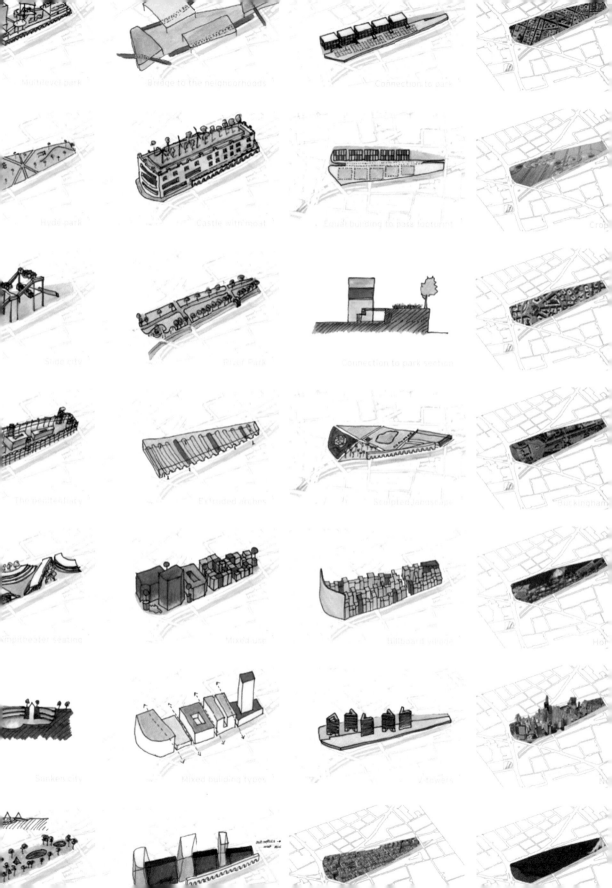

Multilevel park · Bridge to the neighborhoods · Connection to park ·

Hyde park · Castle with moat · Larger building to pass footbridge · Crop

Slide city · River Park · Connection to park section ·

The penitentiary · Extruded arches · Sculpted landscape · Buckingham

Amphitheater seating · Mixed-use · Billboard village · Hou

Sunken city · Mixed building types · Towers ·

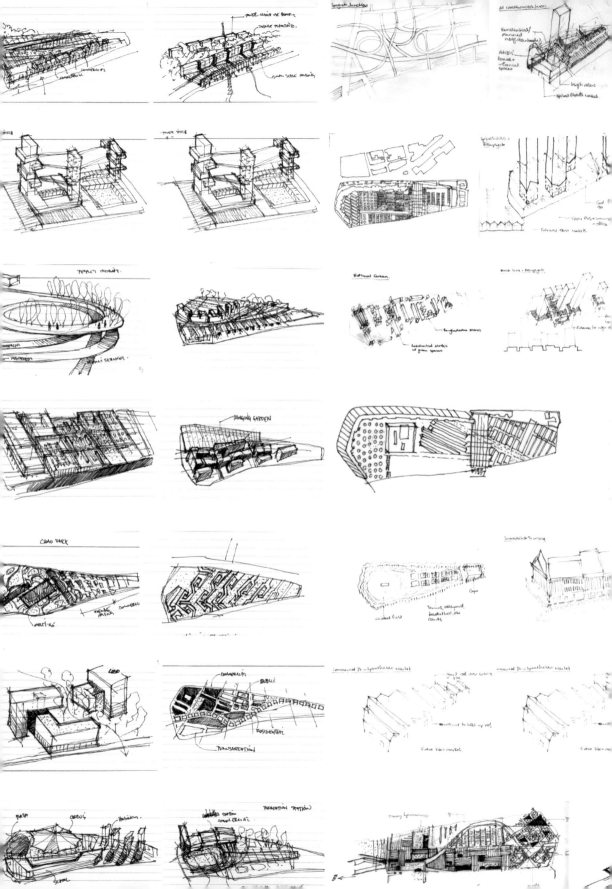

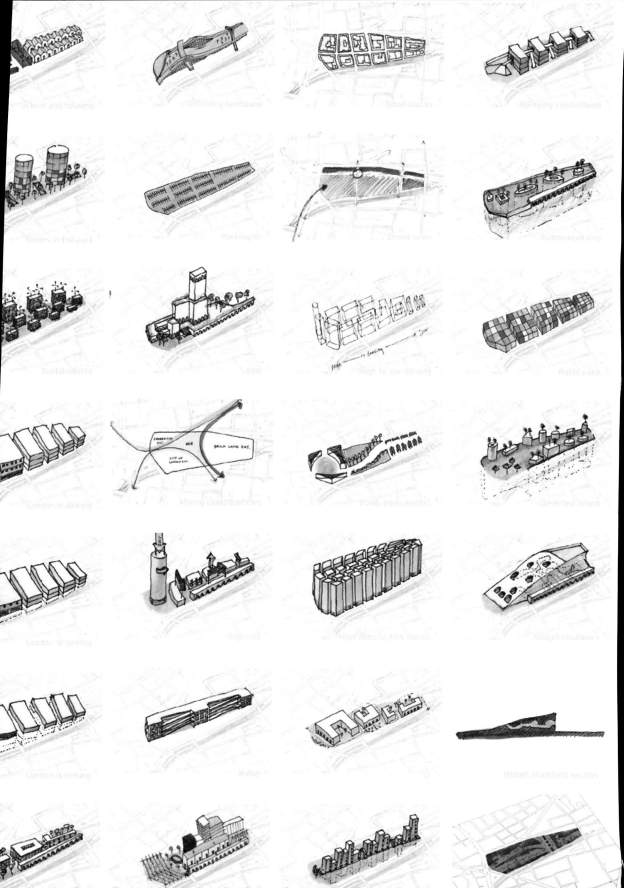

School and housing

Unfolding landscape

Small blocks

Ramping connections

Towers in the park

Parking lot

Street grain

Submerged city

Sustainability

Villa

High to low density

Rubix cube

London is sinking

Mixing constituencies

Pond, park, market

Deserted island

London is sinking

Signage

High density, tiny blocks

Midget chambers

London is sinking

Ramp

Midget chambers section

PROJECTS
STRATEGI

AND S

The Framework Design Exercises established a working method for the studio and set the stage for a weeklong visit to, and investigation of, the site and the surrounding districts (and cultures) of Hoxton, Shoreditch, Brick Lane, and the City, as well as a visit to Manchester to see the work of Urban Splash. Upon their return from England, exploration of the potentials for Bishopsgate Goods Yard began in earnest, as pairs of students developed schemes for the site.

These schemes were not "master plans" per se, but took a form more akin to conceptual visions or frames for thinking about how the site might be organized around various cultures, interests, questions, or architectural languages. Each incorporated a strong thematic or narrative form for a project on the site and used one or several of the tools provided by the framework exercises. Students were asked to produce a single master drawing as well as a short-film animation to explain their project in a mid-semester review.

These conceptual visions were rehearsed and scrutinized at that review, out of which arose myriad questions about each project. Based on this feedback, the students spent a week revising their schemes and, individually, moved on to the more detailed elements of their projects. The fragments re-informed and enriched the overall concepts for the site, resulting in both a generalized urban condition and specific architectural form.

Ruining London: Shelley Zhang and Chiemeka Ejiochi Our project's aim was to challenge the habits of the English Heritage group—a British government agency empowered with the right to designate historically significant structures and impose limits on what the owner may or may not do with such a property. Instead of this traditional method to preserve the historic brick structures on the site, our proposal suggests a way to breathe new life into the old bricks while still paying homage to their historical worth.

Our design involved breaking up the historically significant properties, which often appeared as modern ruins, and redesigning the pieces into new uses suitable for the needed programs on the site. Some of those programmatic features included linking the Shoreditch nightlife at the northwest end of the site with the bustle of Brick Lane, extending Brick Lane's market belt into the site and locating a daycare and fitness center along the western border to tie into the Bishopsgate professional community. "Ruined" building elements were re-appropriated into building façades, market stalls, and public furniture, which were then scattered across the site according to our programmatic analysis. The aim was to transform the site into a sort of allegorical archaeological dig, in which one can burrow through the urban fabric and uncover "archaic" treasures perfectly preserved among the architecture.

By imitating urban forms and weaving in the surrounding city fabric, we added another layer of historical record to the master plan. We even preserved the trace of the Bathwaite brick viaduct arches by employing their original plan on-site. This strategy resulted in a fresh, modern urban attitude that was sensitive to its historical context while keeping in dialogue with the city around it.

Bricolage, as a design tactic, was employed throughout our design process to achieve an effective, cohesive vision. Found elements at both the urban and human scale were altered to develop a new neighborhood. At the city scale, we looked at the solid/void relationship of the surrounding fabric and copied and adapted fragments of it to form new urban spaces. At the smaller scale, identifying and documenting the existing architectural parts found on the site allowed us to start adapting them for new uses. Using these found fragments, we began to alter them to react to modern-day urban needs. Appropriating existing arch fragments into a bench, a bar, or a sun-blocking garden trellis exemplifies the ability to reuse and repurpose this urban ruin.

The goal of the midterm vision was the deployment of newly created brick architectural forms throughout the site. These elements have been distributed across the site based on their programmatic relevance. A pastiche of the old and new, authentic and faux, are planned to the smallest detail and yet seemingly chaotic. It is a microcosm that reflects and absorbs the life of the city surrounding it.

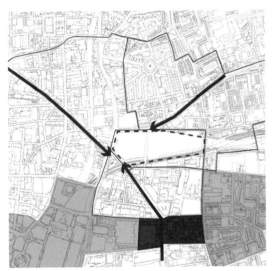

NEIGHBORHOOD LINK

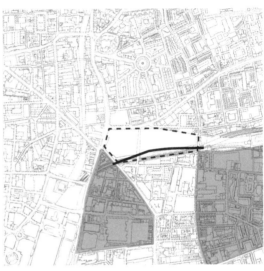

MARKET STREET

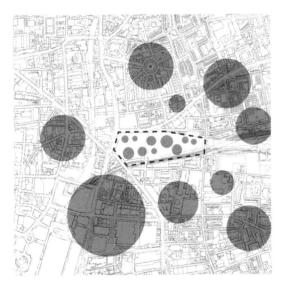

RESIDENTIAL AND COMMERCIAL

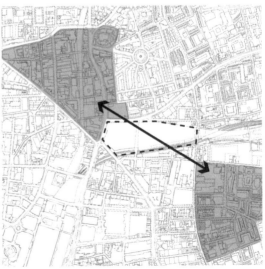

BAR/RESTAURANT CORRIDOR

(Opposite) Connecting the context to the site. (Above) The concept of this project is a vision of the site as a fragment of history, an ancient city in ruins. Such historical sites are carefully conserved in today's society. The project sought to illuminate a new path toward the preservation of the brick structures that had been listed by English Heritage. The aim was to breathe new life into the old bricks while still respecting their historical value.

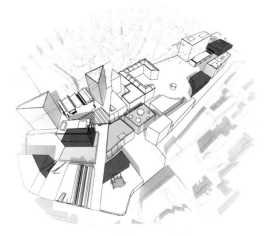

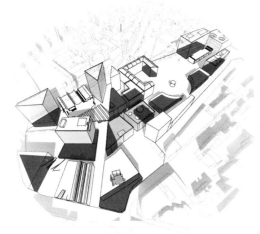

Distribution of programs also is determined by occupancy type and size. All types are equally distributed across the area to produce a consistently active environment.

Susan Yelavich: The idea of the ruin can be thought of in terms of urban decay, in that you are building a ruin, which is already partly decayed because—"ashes to ashes." If the city is immortal, we are immortal.

Fred Tang: One also has to address what is the meaning of decay or the feeling of distress or the feeling of fragmentation.

John McMorrough: You've looked at it very closely in terms of the typologies of display that are created from the ruin, but another set of diagrams could describe the re-inhabitation of ruins, which would allow you to be precise with the deployments. I wonder, is this building a ruin of a future we haven't had yet?

Kieran Long: There was a lot more to Bishopsgate Goods Yard before they started demolishing it. There is not much left to be fetishized. It starts to sound ironic in an uncomfortable way, not in a humorous way, when you end up fetishizing something that is already gone.

Charles Holland: You treat the ruin in many different manifestations. Sometimes it's literal, sometimes it's a weird shape you've extruded, and sometimes it's a new thing built to look like a ruin. There is a slippery proliferation of tactics used here that makes your stance on the ruin unclear.

Sean Griffiths: Part of the aim is to try to capture something poetic while at the same time trying to deal with the reality that this is a bit of city and not just a surrealist's playground.

John McMorrough: The emphasis on ruin has been at the level of "fragment," at the level of "building." At midterm you showed one model of a ruin, which was picturesque fragments spread across a field. Another series of diagrams could investigate what that field of the ruin is. The ruin could be the re-importation of fragments onto a site. The ruin could be an original urban fabric that has been degraded but that you can still move through, like the Roman Forum, which is partially restricted. There are conceptual models that deal in different ways with the ruin at the level of a fragment and at the level of a plan.

Mimi Zeiger: I like the area in which you have taken a diagonal across the site. This connective tissue is something we have not seen in previous schemes. You have begun to carve out of the site rather than cutting it to the bone.

Elihu Rubin: You have an intuitive sense for how this part of the site works, shown by where that diagonal street cuts through. The urbanism of the street, the buildings, and even playing with those façades potentially moves you into a very large, open public space.

ARCH / DOOR   VIADUCT / RETAIL   ARCH / WINDOW   VIADUCT / PLAY   ARCH / TRELLIS

VIADUCT / TROUGH   ARCH / FAÇADE 1   VIADUCT / BOOTH   ARCH / FAÇADE 2   VIADUCT / BRIDGE

ARCH / BENCH   VIADUCT / FAÇADE   ARC / ARCADE   VIADUCT / SEATING   ARCH / FAÇADE 4

VIADUCT / GATE   ARCH / GLORIFIED RUIN   VIADUCT / PLANTERS   ARCH / MARKET   ARCH / FAÇADE 3

ARCH / BLACKBOARD   ARCH / BAR   VIADUCT / KIOSK   VIADUCT / INFO BOOTH   ARCH / BILLBOARD

A typology of ruins, these ruins are fragmented, broken down into their lowest common denominators, and completely taken out of their original context, freeing them to be appropriated for other uses.

Emmanuel Petit: There seems to be a difference between the accumulation of fragments, which just become autonomous fragments sitting next to each other, and the fragmentation of a scheme that was once an overall scheme. One wonders, if this is the ruination of an absolute scheme, what was the absolute scheme in the first place? It doesn't seem to build up to anything bigger than just the fragmentation of different ideas being clustered together.

Fred Tang: I think we all see ruins in terms of this formal ruin, or the aesthetic of a ruin. Everybody keeps talking about this as a figure-ground—we expect to see an erosion of the figure or ground. But I think we also need to talk about the program and what is a ruin of a program. Or is there a way to re-inhabit the forms with new program? Is there a typology of a house which, using program, you take the ruin of a house and put a museum in it or vice versa? You have housing at the top, and it looks like an apartment building. There is no sense of a programmatic ruin, which is part of what I would expect in a project that deals with fragmentation.

John McMorrough: The site plan is really an accommodation of particularities. I don't think there's an overall scheme in so much as there are episodic moments that are pulled together by building. I am quite interested in that as an approach because you can basically instrumentalize yourself at different moments in the urban fabric, but then I do think this notion of the overall plan could come in.

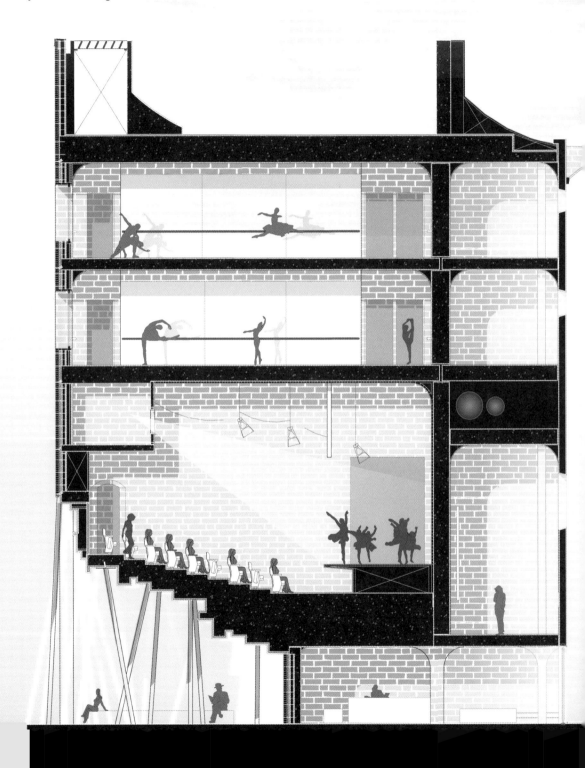

The structure of this dance studio and performing-arts center is supported on steel pilotis. The façade is constructed using reappropriated bricks from the site. Bricks appear to crumble away to reveal views of dancers practicing inside.

Magnetic Attraction: Lydia Miller and Christopher Corbett This project connects two adjacent neighborhoods through a corridor that cuts across the site. While still catering to the day users of London's financial district by providing office and commercial space, the neighborhoods of Brick Lane at the east and Shoreditch at the northwest will benefit through additional housing and commercial and arts programming proliferating on the site.

The site attracts people to pass through this all-important arts corridor by locating two areas of open space with adjacent "programmatic magnets" at either end of the site. These magnets at the poles are pockets of dense activity and program, accommodating multiple functions in a single structure.

On the west end of the site, the loop tower uses water as the driving narrative to create a vertical community. The goal of this exercise is to identify links between a broad set of programs through their water uses. The juxtaposition of a variety of programs, from student housing and a laundromat to office space, forefronts the common need for water. Whether it is for dormitory showers, washing machines, or tempering the interiors of large office spaces, water is a necessity for life and can bring together different contingencies. The relationships found through programmatic juxtaposition play off cultural norms and allow for new types of adjacencies, that find commonalities through this often hidden commodity. By exposing the collection, storage, filtration, and use of water as a common denominator, new spatial relationships can be articulated. Rather than define edges, this juxtaposition exposes the overlaps among different social groups.

Clusters of programmatic families are tied together through this central theme. Water has a transformative power beyond its typical use and becomes a form of capital, figuratively and literally. A gym, brewery, spa, laundromat, and park have been introduced into the residential towers to act as the network's nodes, collectively demonstrating the importance water has in the rituals of life, ranging from the functional to the spiritual. Collected water is treated biologically in the park, then stored in large tanks that simultaneously cool the office spaces. The brewery uses the water to produce beer, and the waste hops are used to grow mushrooms. Each part contributes and benefits from the hydrologic cycle, allowing the buildings to function as a whole, socially and physically.

The eastern magnet borrows the row-house typology ubiquitously found in the Brick Lane area and reshuffles the typical distribution of program within it. Using the design tactic of appropriation, this building takes its form from the local building stock but shakes up its insides, creating new juxtapositions of program.

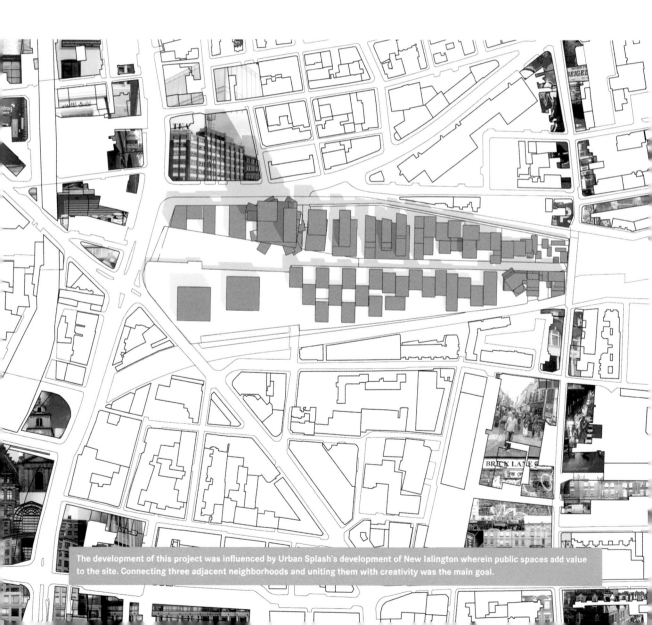

The development of this project was influenced by Urban Splash's development of New Islington wherein public spaces add value to the site. Connecting three adjacent neighborhoods and uniting them with creativity was the main goal.

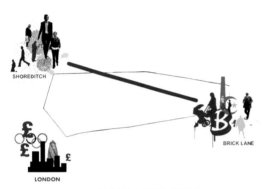

1. CREATIVE CONNECTION

2. CREATIVE CORRIDOR

3. CREATIVE CORRIDOR

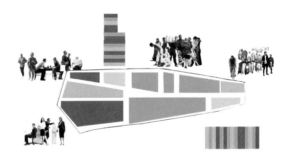

4. PUBLIC SPACES ■
MIXED RESIDENTIAL ■
COMMERCIAL ■
PROGRAM MAGNET ■

1. A pedestrian street would connect two neighborhoods that both have a creative presence. 2. Adjusting the street makes use of the site's existing viaduct structure. 3. This pedestrian street will be lined with arts programs for a cohesive and vibrant new art community. 4. Commercial space is located adjacent to the financial district, and residential space fills the rest of the site. Public open space is paired with dense program magnets at the periphery of the development to bring people through the site.

Rather than the prescriptive mixed-use doctrine of commercial on the ground level and residential above, the block-long structure combines activities such as a community theater, laundromat, mosque, and housing for the elderly into a new, chaotic organization. Interesting adjacencies emerge and environmental connections are used to coalesce this magnet into a single attraction.

The appropriation of the housing typology from Brick Lane allows the adjacent urban fabric to penetrate into the site while still creating a new kind of building through its interior organization. Placing a great variety of programs within this magnet at the eastern pole of the site encourages people from the neighboring area to visit. It is hoped the arts corridor will inspire people to enter deeper into the site and experience a new neighborhood rich in culture.

Frank Lupo: This is an extremely audacious combination of program. The point is to get them to all work for the transportation. It is also very intriguing to see how the typology of a family-dwelling level differs from the typology of the interior. You're enticing us with this wonderful vertical sandwich, but I would love to see how the vertical innovation translates to the interconnectedness of the plan.

John McMorrough: How the program attractors operate vis-à-vis the rest of the development on your site and also in terms of the urban fabric as a whole? You have an intense collage of color and form, and so on, and it makes quite a difference in the urban landscape. But is the rest of your development on the site more of what we see everywhere else, so that it blends in, or is the whole zone a special thing? You have taken on the pervasive materiality of Brick Lane, which is brick. I am curious about your program magnet, but it seems that there is some sort of visualization going on, too.

Lydia Miller: Starting with the typology of Brick Lane, the materiality reads as a whole as though there are various different programs inside; it is functioning as a unit. I used the exterior fenestration to code the interior program.

John McMorrough: Street elevations would give you a sense of how that difference plays against the fabric. Does the syncopation of the different fenestrations register a difference in the urban fabric?

Mimi Zeiger: I think the rear of the building tells the story about what occurs inside, with the screen of the mosque, the theater space jutting out, and the laundry above, but you are being very restricted on the street side.

Michael Speaks: You mentioned Richard Florida buzz words with "creative lane." But how do these strategies differ from Foster's? How did you come up with the programs that you included as program magnets, and how do you think they work with one another?

Chris Corbett: I started with a typical mixed residential tower, with residential on the top, then office, and then commercial and retail at the bottom. Then I began splitting the residential into more specific sections so it became the family, the student, and the more expensive units.

John McMorrough: If this is an intensification of what would typically happen, then it comes down to not only the way in which the programs are visualized in terms of their massing or their appearance but also the way they are realized in terms of the inhabitation of the building. It is really staged quite discretely into different zones. It is programmatic, but it is also visual and experiential in terms of the internal life of

TWIN KIDS   CRICKET   LONELY   CONSUMPTIVE   FOOD   FURNITURE   UNSTABLE   IMMIGRANT   GAY   HOMELESS
             BROTHERS   NOVEL   ARTIST   BLOGGER   BUILDER   LOVERS   STORE   CONSTRUCTION INVESTOR
                        READER   OWNER   WORKER

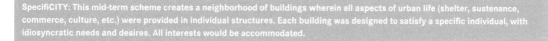

SpecifiCITY: This mid-term scheme creates a neighborhood of buildings wherein all aspects of urban life (shelter, sustenance, commerce, culture, etc.) were provided in individual structures. Each building was designed to satisfy a specific individual, with idiosyncratic needs and desires. All interests would be accommodated.

The open space on the east end provides a place for the Brick Lane market to overflow, bringing people into and through the site.

the building. Right now I see them as very different encoded worlds, and I don't see when those worlds collide or where you start to appreciate the difference. It doesn't use the means of the building type to stage or highlight these differences.

Fred Tang: The project actually provides opposites in terms of programmatic mixing. Lydia has this sort of anti-representational program that looks very plain on the outside and could fit right in. It almost looks Modern or New Urbanist in its contextualism, but on the inside there is operational program mixing in which laundry rooms look over into theaters and houses look over into fly towers. On the other hand, Chris has representational program mixing in a heterogeneity, but the stacking is kind of anti-mixing. By keeping everything in its own sort of stacked world there is no interaction between them.

Mimi Zeiger: Between your two buildings, there is all this other program. Is that designed, or is that more like what is already there?

Lydia Miller: Richard Florida writes about the importance of creative industry and how it makes for a vibrant city, which he statistically backs up. Along this creative corridor, the ground-level space would be arts/retail space or arts-based programs. This is different from Foster's scheme in which there might be some of this program sporadically placed on the site, but it is not set up financially. The more profitable programs at the west end of the site can actually support the arts programming. Since midterm we have thought about creating one building for one person that would encompass everything they need; so it would have housing, it would have occupation, and it would have retail elements—fundamentally trying to create a city within a building.

Kieran Long: It is interesting to discuss towers in the U.S. because there are no mixed-use towers in the U.K. that I can think of; it's not the kind of thing we do. I mean a multiprogrammatic sandwich might seem kind of banal here, but in London it might be potentially more interesting. I question your understanding of the context. You perceive Brick Lane and Shoreditch as being two kinds of arts hubs in a Richard Florida way, which I find slightly unsettling. One reason Shoreditch is an arts hub is because of the consistent mismanagement of the real estate stock by the local authority.

Susan Yelavich: Could zoning permit people to grow these buildings by allowing add-ons?

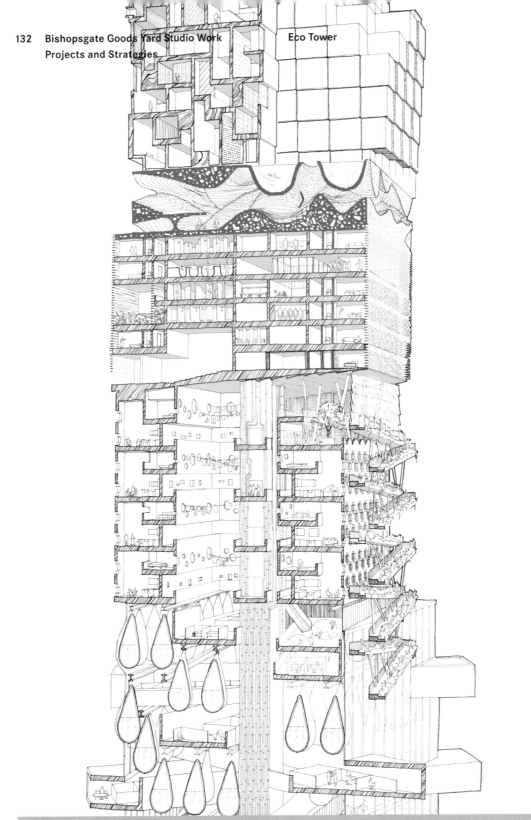

Section through the western program magnet in which the vertical stacking of program creates interesting juxtapositions that inform the architecture and the environmental systems.

Elihu Rubin: I have an appealing feeling now about planning for mismanagement. Maybe that is actually the best way to go, as opposed to overplanning or overmanagement. There would be much more room for flexibility and growth. I think your project raises the larger issue: can this be planned? There's top-down, bottom-up, and just bottom. How do you connect the bottom to some sort of strategic vision? It takes time. Maybe this arts corridor is precisely the kind of area that artists would want to avoid. Or maybe they will be strolling in this area because it represents exactly the kinds of forces for those kinds of places to operate.

Patrick Bellew: What you haven't really dealt with in that tower, which is a big challenge when you try to mix uses, is how to manage daylighting. Some of these spaces that you infer were lighted well; they are actually solid at the top and don't link through to the "glass house" or the "living machine" and would actually be dark spaces.

The plaza on the west end will draw people from London and Shoreditch into the arts corridor and the large program magnet.

A section through the eastern program magnet shows the density and variety of program within the building. A mosque, laundromat, artist loft, apartments, and community theater co-exist within the same brick shell, interacting physically, visually, and environmentally.

BUCKLE, SPAM and the City: Nicholas W. McDermott and Elizabeth McDonald The nature of London's open spaces has been compromised by the corporate ownership of plazas and courtyards. Such ownership creates ambiguous relationships between the public and private realms that, in turn, constrain behavior and put limits on the kinds of conduct that are acceptable in these spaces. Could a Frisbee toss take place in the plaza beneath a corporate high-rise? Not really, and yet this is almost the only kind of public space currently found in the financial district, the commercial heart of London that forms the southern edge of our site.

We put forth the radical proposition of offering the Bishopsgate neighborhood some real public space, the kind that allows for a breadth of activities, unconstrained by category and marked by the potential for spontaneity. The proposal calls for a mix of new commercial and residential buildings interwoven with sports and recreation areas, plots for urban agriculture, and a small forested park, as well as a proposal for a museum and housing complex—the Shoreditch Printed Arts Museum (SPAM)—dedicated to the preservation of the neighborhood's history as a center of the printed arts. A building constructed out of a part of the historic Braithwaite viaduct will define the eastern edge of the site immediately adjacent to the lively foot traffic on Brick Lane—the city's epicenter of South Asian culture—and will house a cooking school and curry museum called BUCKLE, the Bangladeshi Urban Curry Kitchen of London, England.

By overlaying a variety of uses and people onto a single space we are able to create a more diverse and interesting urban condition. The BUCKLE Building weaves together layers of residential garden terraces, markets, classrooms, and restaurants into a new type of live/work/eat building while blurring the accepted boundaries of public and private spaces through its circulation. The SPAM Building continues to blend these once rigid divisions by bringing the public space literally up the façade of the building. Pockets of public activity erode into the building at various heights, including high in the sky. A continuum of public space at the ground level allows people to flow through and between buildings, deconstructing the norm of restrictive "public" plazas surrounding private office buildings and permitting a new flow to be established.

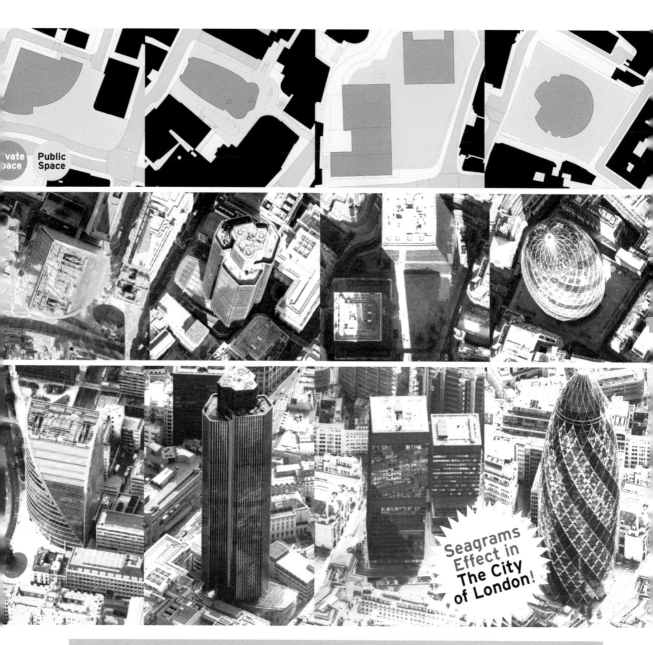

London's financial district on the southwestern edge of the site has a large number of plazas, courtyards, and alleys that are privately owned or maintained. We call this dichotomy of privately controlled public space the "Seagram effect."

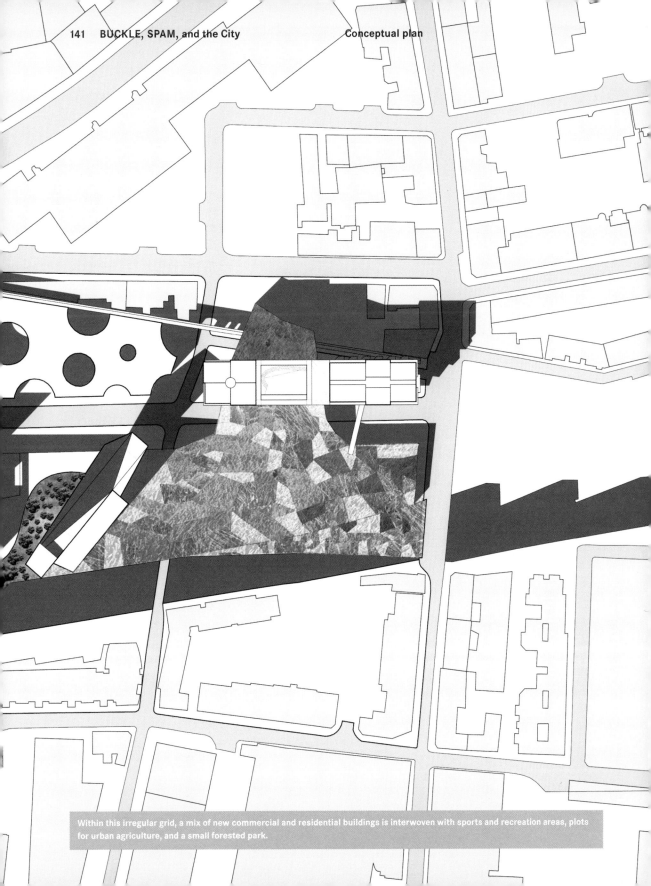

Within this irregular grid, a mix of new commercial and residential buildings is interwoven with sports and recreation areas, plots for urban agriculture, and a small forested park.

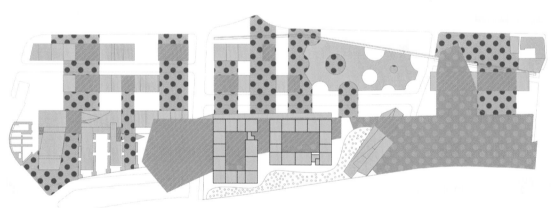

BUILDING ENVELOPE   INTERIOR SPACE

PUBLIC PROGRAM   EXTERIOR SPACE

(Above) Public and private program are woven over the site, creating overlaps and layers. Building envelopes are manipulated to expand the boundaries of public space from a flat plane into thickened layers. (Opposite) The program is distributed on the site with a large number of residences and park space being added to the dense east end, as well as more retail and work space at the west end.

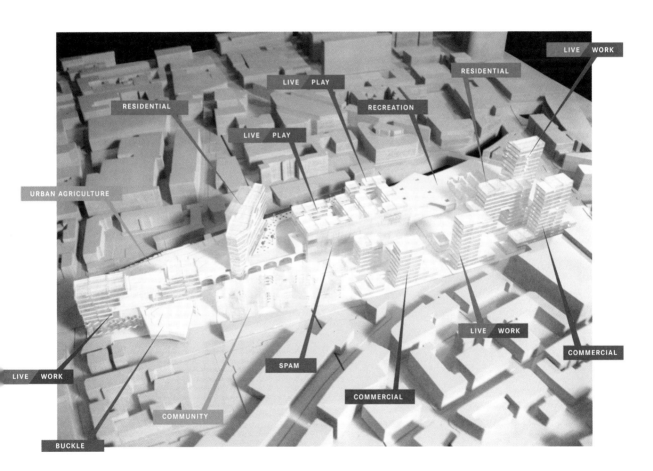

BUCKLE, the Bangladeshi Urban Curry Kitchen of London, England, is a cooking school and curry museum constructed out of the remaining segments of the historic Braithwaite viaduct.

Robert Stern: Where would you place your scheme in the history of post–World War II urbanism?

Nicholas McDermott: It is an alternative to buildings such as the Seagram Building, in which there is an attempt to give public space back to the public but not ending up where we are now, which is the Foster scheme of corporatized public spaces.

Robert Stern: The large-scale plan you have—elevated above the street, with no streets or clear circulation within the building area, with a strange landscape and towers that seem to have no sense of bounding space—strikes me as a typical urban renewal scheme that dates from World War II until about the 1970s, when people said they had had enough of it. Some buildings have been torn down, some have been ameliorated in some way or another, and a few have actually earned their way into the affections of people, like the one in London, the Barbican.

Nicholas McDermott: The spaces like Spitalfields Market, which are gloomy but well used and well loved, fascinate us.

Kieran Long: Spitalfields Market has a street façade, which makes it a street, and behind that street façade is a large kind of space that is used in many different ways.

Susan Yelavich: The verticality of the Seagram model is not compromised here. If in fact the site is a center and the buildings become jungle gyms for the public, then the roof garden becomes a public space—this is the proposition. I don't think it's necessarily a viable model, but I think it's a catalyst for thinking about buildings differently.

John McMorrough: You have done a good job packaging ideas into comprehensible forms. I think there is more to be done with the Seagram effect than "public is horizontal, private is vertical." I think already in the Seagram model there is an implicit economic and political model as well. The Seagram effect is the effect of the corporation creating that space. You have to acknowledge that there was first a creation of space within the city; it ended up being a corporate kind of space, but there was an accomplishment to that model that introduced openness to the city. Already there is a model of exchange implied with that. I am missing a second iteration of the Seagram effect in which there would be a system of exchange you could play on. Right now it's taken formally, but it could use an economic method of exchange that could mobilize on the site.

Michael Speaks: It seems as if you're taking one measure and using that measure to create an entire strategic intervention, but I don't see how it works, except that you've observed you don't like the Seagram effect, and you've cleared out two buildings. What is the bigger picture and the strategy?

Charles Holland: The isolated monument for the project is the tall building, but then there is a vacuous space around it, which is presumably part of what you were reacting against in the Seagram Building's urban plaza.

Elihu Rubin: I don't read this as monuments in a vacuum. In fact, there's tremendous potential, particularly in remaking streets and streetscapes. To me, that is engaging. There are streets and potential streets. Seagram's strategy of public space to me is okay. What is so bad about essentially having a building that's private and having a well-designed public space in front of it that is well used? I wonder if these public spaces inserted at the street face of a private building are destined never to be truly public.

Kieran Long: The question is, then, what constitutes a public space? Now it's becoming a kind of question of semantics. To me, it has to be tied to something. I think my cards are slightly on the table in this regard, but what you perceive as the Seagram effect is the separation of the public and private realm so that those two things don't interact programmatically. Your solution is to weave them together somehow but to potentially still have a vertical configuration. Richard Sennett, the sociologist, attributes the failure of the ground-floor space of the Seagram Building to the Modernist language being unable to charge that space with any sort of character, i.e., typological archetypal, architectural use. So there may be other factors contributing to the public/private dichotomy that you alter to break down this effect.

Robert Stern: It is private space in which the public is allowed to go across. It is very different from the many hundreds that followed.

Susan Yelavich: This is a critique of the dominance of the corporate presence. It is more semiotic. It may not be an effective architecture and urban solution. The semiotic information here is fairly powerful.

Emmanuel Petit: I am troubled by the shopping-mall approach to urbanism. I realize when Koolhaas did his Exodus project and transferred the Berlin Wall to London in order to give an island an oasis of bliss to all these bored Londoners, that trope is still active. It seems like we are thinking of urbanism as a series of features that are somehow activating our short attention span and making the urban space a little bit like

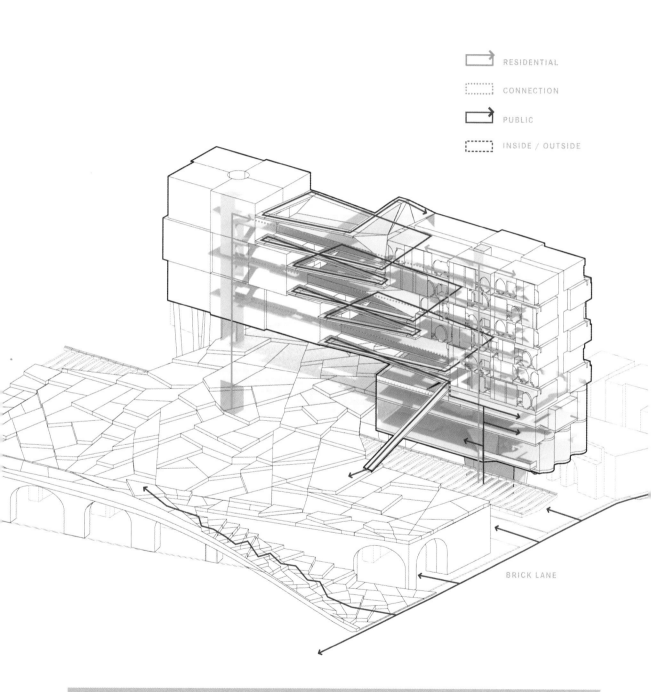

RESIDENTIAL

CONNECTION

PUBLIC

INSIDE / OUTSIDE

BRICK LANE

A public room adjacent to the gardens and restaurants at the base of BUCKLE winds its way up through the building to an amphitheater and public market at the roof.

TV's—"Oh, look here!" and "Something is happening here!" and "My kids can play here"—but is that the kind of approach we want for urbanism?

Susan Yelavich: I see something else: it is cutting wormholes through public space in different ways, conceptually, to create private spaces. In other words, we accept our environment as being dictated by money and that it's not going to stop, so let's work with it differently.

Emmanuel Petit: It is so dictated by capitalism that I would want to put graffiti all over it.

Robert Stern: The great public spaces of a city—and London is one of the world's greatest cities—are its streets. They're fantastic public spaces. So the more streets you have and the more different ways they let you go, presumably the more freedom you would experience.

Kieran Long: When the Smithsons did their photography work on the streets of east London with Nigel Henderson they became very interested in the slums because these streets were not-programmed-at-all places, with social exchange as places of genuine publicness in the city. They were uncatagorizable and unprogrammed, and that was their quality.

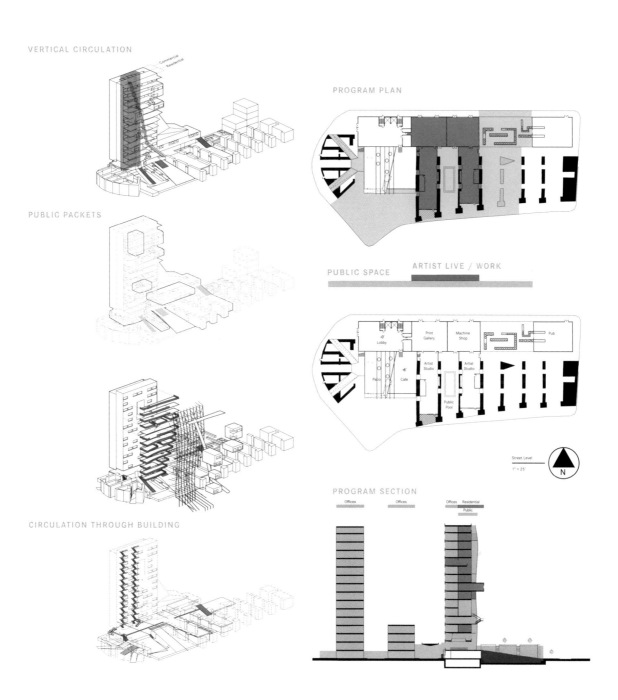

VERTICAL CIRCULATION

PUBLIC PACKETS

CIRCULATION THROUGH BUILDING

PROGRAM PLAN

PUBLIC SPACE   ARTIST LIVE / WORK

PROGRAM SECTION

A new live/work building challenges the essential nature of boundaries between public and private realms by folding the surrounding community park up and into the building envelope.

The building grafts live spaces with work spaces, then overlays that traditional combination of program with a public structure allowing for movement up the building's exterior, creating the façade.

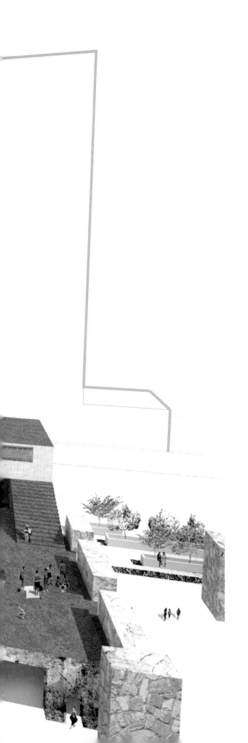

Spectacular Vernacular: Gabrielle Ho and Christina Wu In the surrounding areas of the Bishopsgate Goods Yard site, buildings have been reappropriated over time as London tries to retain its historical character while keeping up with modern needs. Our project simulates this phenomenon by clashing together familiar building types and redefining the relationships among scale, materials, program, and styles. As new relationships are formed, certain associations are retained in order to evoke the memory of each building typology's origin. The intention is to challenge people's visual and social habits by causing them to pause and reconsider their understanding of common things. The result is a spectacle that draws on ideas about the vernacular and addresses the relationship between high and low culture.

The design tactic of appropriation was used as the basis of this project. Starting with typical building forms, materials, and styles found around the site and throughout London, we began to alter the architecture to create something new. By tripling the scale of a window, casting old wooden shingles out of concrete, or cutting a section through a building and cladding it with glass, we sought to make the local visitor re-evaluate their presumptions about architecture. At the scale of the neighborhood, this effect was achieved through grander gestures of colliding whole buildings together to create a massing island of architecture. Where these buildings intersect, the common spaces can be used in a variety of ways: exterior façades can protrude into the interior of lobbies, whole rooms can be created, or circulation space can be defined. Within the "island," one typology devours another, and a new spatial relationship results. This appropriation of our accepted typologies creates an environment to which we can relate but still makes us question our urban understanding.

Section cuts are revealed and become the street façades along some of the streets leading into the site.

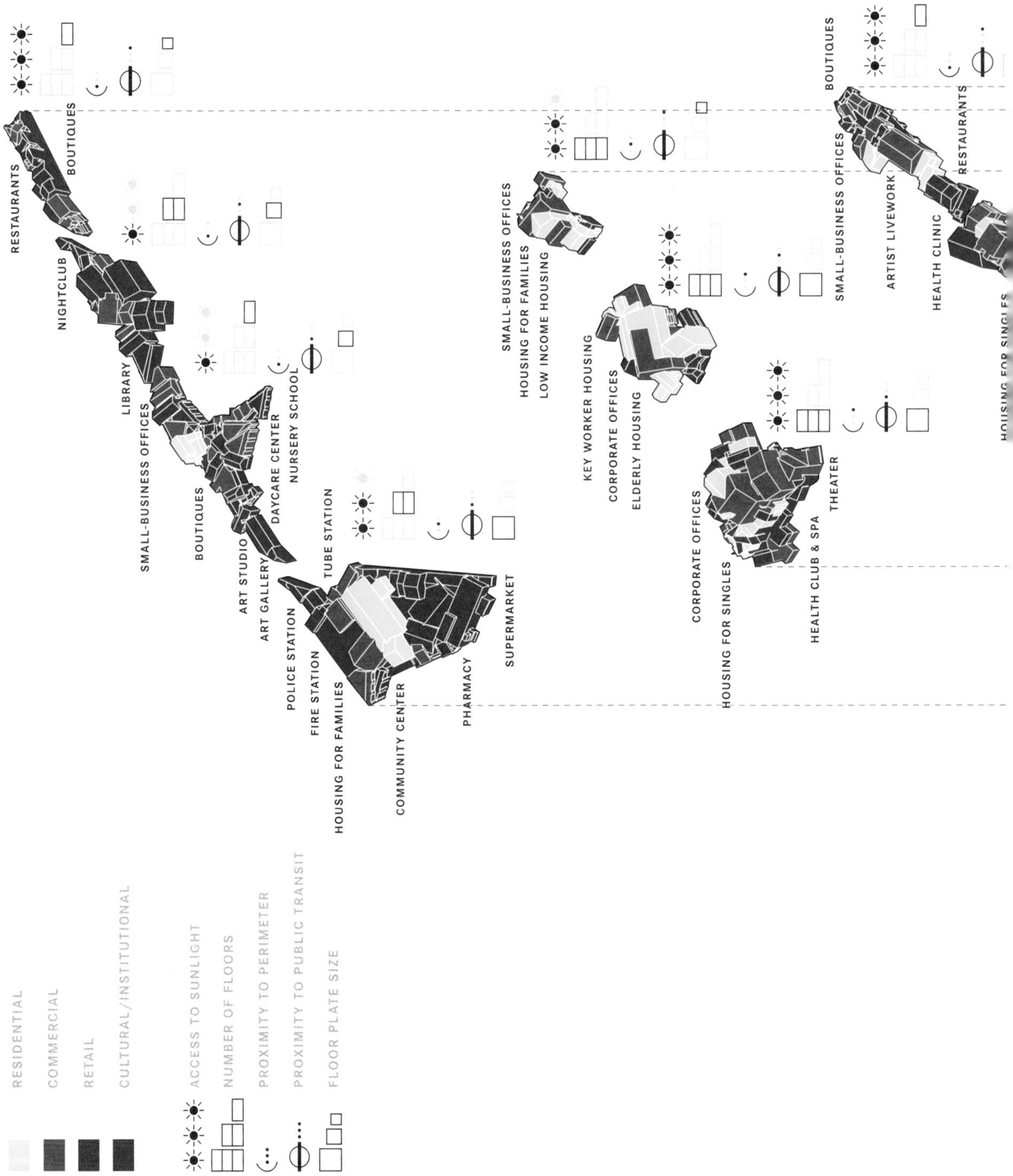

RESTAURANTS

BOUTIQUES

NIGHTCLUB

LIBRARY

SMALL-BUSINESS OFFICES

BOUTIQUES

ART STUDIO

ART GALLERY

DAYCARE CENTER

NURSERY SCHOOL

TUBE STATION

POLICE STATION

FIRE STATION

HOUSING FOR FAMILIES

COMMUNITY CENTER

PHARMACY

SUPERMARKET

SMALL-BUSINESS OFFICES

HOUSING FOR FAMILIES

LOW INCOME HOUSING

KEY WORKER HOUSING

CORPORATE OFFICES

ELDERLY HOUSING

CORPORATE OFFICES

HOUSING FOR SINGLES

HEALTH CLUB & SPA

THEATER

BOUTIQUES

RESTAURANTS

SMALL-BUSINESS OFFICES

ARTIST LIVEWORK

HEALTH CLINIC

HOUSING FOR SINGLES

RESIDENTIAL

COMMERCIAL

RETAIL

CULTURAL/INSTITUTIONAL

ACCESS TO SUNLIGHT

NUMBER OF FLOORS

PROXIMITY TO PERIMETER

PROXIMITY TO PUBLIC TRANSIT

FLOOR PLATE SIZE

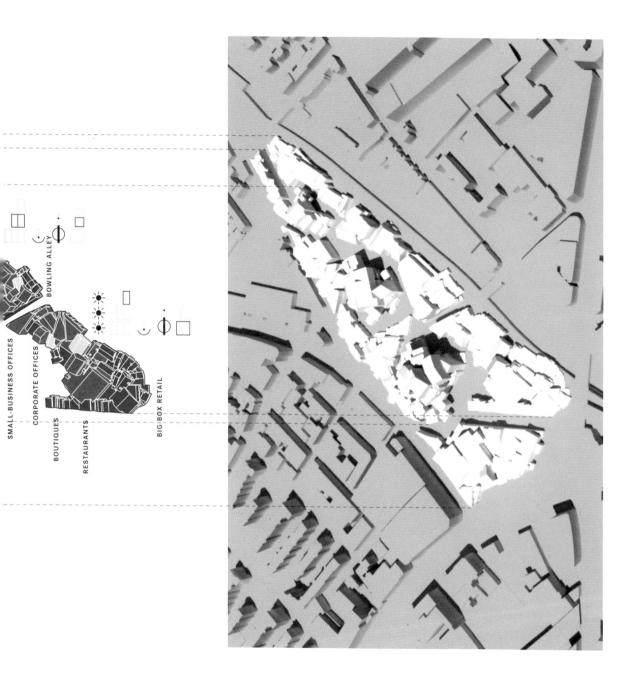

SMALL-BUSINESS OFFICES
CORPORATE OFFICES
BOWLING ALLEY
BOUTIQUES
RESTAURANTS
BIG-BOX RETAIL

The program on the site is distributed to maximize mix, permitting close proximity of one type of program next to another. The diagram maps each area's access to sunlight, number of floors, proximity to perimeter, proximity to public transit, and floor-plate size. Studying the context helps determine where to reveal sections relative to routes into and through the site.

The site plan at the section cut shows a variety of surface textures and an open plaza space.

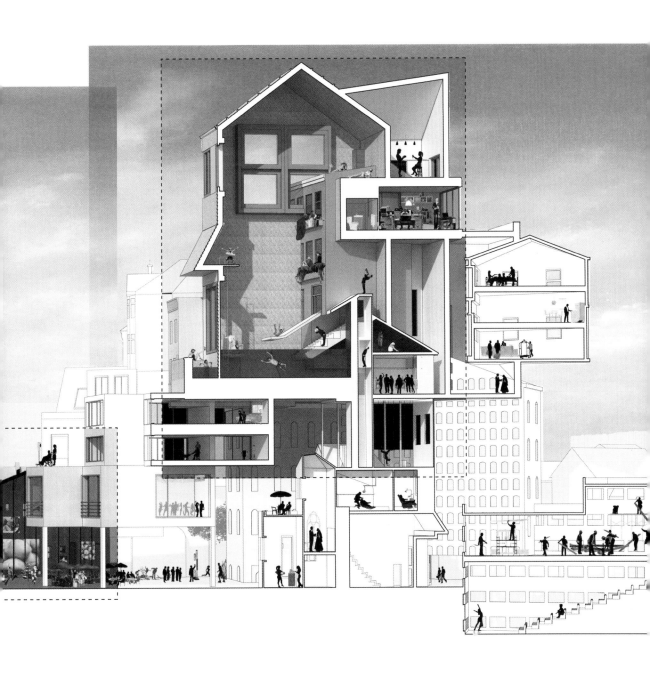

This part of London has incredible diversity of program. By mashing together familiar, easily recognized volumes and distorting them in scale and orientation, new relationships and interesting spaces result.

CROSS-SECTION THROUGH PERIMETER, ONE INTERNAL ISLAND, AND RAILROAD TRACKS

PUBLICLY ACCESSED ROAD

PERIMETER WITH FAMILIAR FAÇADE FACING THE STREET

GLAZING ON BUILDINGS WITH SECTION CUTS
AS ENTRY POINTS INTO MASTER PLAN

John McMorrough: When you say you are interested in playing with expectations, what does that do? Taking that as a kind of performative potential, what do these new relationships and forms do for urban life? What do they mobilize in habitation?

Christina Wu: There is a tension and surprise in which the reveal evokes surprise. That surprise, whether it is a good reaction or a negative reaction, doesn't matter. We just want to galvanize an emotional response to what one expects. This design incorporates a variety from inside to outside, creating an interesting way to add life to the site for the people who already live there and for visitors.

Michael Speaks: What happens the second time you see it?

Christina Wu: Hopefully, you will stumble upon something you didn't expect to see the first time, because there is a lot going on. The building typologies we chose were influenced by what we saw around the site. Exploring the terrace housing and the big warehouses in terms of the way they are massed on the site, we wanted it to be a diagram of the perimeter that then gained height as you went in. The slits are located relative to the connection that we want to make from Bethnal Green down to Shoreditch High Street. Then we use a commercial road connection to bring you in.

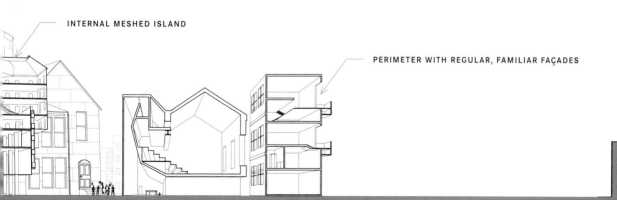

INTERNAL MESHED ISLAND

PERIMETER WITH REGULAR, FAMILIAR FAÇADES

Various façade treatments are used to either expose the section of a building or its interior spaces or to disguise a space behind the faux façades.

Façade animation

FAKE FAÇADE HIDES OPEN SPACES

GLAZING ON FAÇADE REVEALS INTERIOR

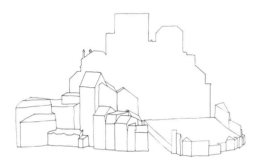

HIDDEN RECTANGULAR BUILDING

SECTION CUT OF BUILDING EXPRESSED ON FAÇADE

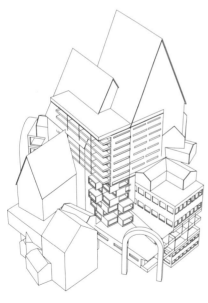

MASSING FOR INTERNAL ISLAND

(Top) Multiple façade treatments were employed to expose a building's interior space or its section. Other elevations used faux façades to create a false perception of the building's true nature. (Bottom) Floor plates were stacked and twisted to create a new way of massing, blurring the boundaries between one structure and another.

Emmanuel Petit: What goes into the mishmash? Because it seems like you don't have only tomatoes and carrots and stuff, but each one of these is genetically modified. The roof of the tower seems Scandinavian to me, not from this neighborhood. The window in the other tower seems Rossi-esque or maybe Venturi-esque, certainly not London-esque. This makes me question what the ingredients are for your mishmash.

Gabrielle Ho: It used to be a form that was found around the perimeter of the site. We were interested in the materiality and the scale because we wanted to turn it into something vaguely familiar and surprising at the same time.

Christina Wu: It may reference sites outside of London, but our intention is for the trim details, doors, and forms to be of the area.

Robert Stern: I think it is very London. It looks very logical to me. It has streets and blocks, and it has a way to address the edges at a scale that I think is complementary, and then in the center it rises up to bigger buildings. This produces the density necessary to satisfy the greed factor for the people who own the land, and it gives people a variety of ways to live.

Fred Tang: There's a great amount of delight at your level of perversity. You answer the question of "What does brick want to be?" and we had no idea it wanted to be a wood shingle.

Kieran Long: I am interested in the answer to the question, what about the second time? The crushing together of something that is apparently typological with something that is overtly sensational, which is about surprising someone, obviously has a limited life span. If what you're trying to do is to be sensational, to provide something unexpected, then it can be unexpected only once, and then thereafter, what? You've done a very interesting polemical thing by separating those things entirely, but I wonder from where that sensational situation comes? It's like Disneyland or Vegas; it could just as easily be anything on the inside to you.

Robert Stern: In citing those two places, you are citing the two most successful urban environments that have been conceived by the normal development process since World War II in the entire world.

Kieran Long: Well, it depends on how one measures success.

Robert Stern: No, people like it. The world is divided between architects and real people.

Kieran Long: I think what we have is something undeniably of character, a character which is almost the bore at the dinner table. You would have them at the dinner table, but you probably wouldn't have them every week.

Robert Stern: I think if we go beyond the forms here, there is a solid idea. There are people sitting, facing what looks like a sidewalk, which is facing a street. That is an urban idea. Here are people actually able to walk from the street, get off the bus, and go into the place. That is maybe a 2,000-year-old urban idea but given a new spin in a new place, and that works.

Kieran Long: It is imagery of something chaotic and organic that is in fact highly contrived—not that contrived is bad.

John McMorrough: I want to appreciate the project precisely on this issue of contrivance. You argue in terms of surprise and revelation and creating a new cognition of a city, but that is not what I find interesting about it. The question that the studio poses is, how can the master plan have the appearance or effect of spontaneity of life without contrivance? You have offered some rather rudimentary shapes or forms through a permeation of scale and overlap, and you can generate the affect of spontaneity, the affect of liveliness. For me, it breaks down when you don't know how to resolve it conceptually. What I really love in the section and what I love about the project in general can be seen in the theater above. You have removed the signification from the appearance of the form from what's happening within. What was a single-family row house can become the theater, and then through shrinkage it can become a rehearsal room.

Robert Stern: I would use the word *unplanning*. It's a great concept.

Kieran Long: But it's highly specific.

Robert Stern: But the effect is that it was never planned. That is something that has eluded most planning efforts for a very long time.

Elihu Rubin: The model gives me the impression that you have these ideas with respect to materiality and form, and that this will actually grow as a kind of ad hoc kind of community. That could not possibly be the actual proposal, however. This is just one build-out.

John McMorrough: It is precisely the possibility that it could be built out in one step that makes me appreciate this scheme. The intellectual challenge is, how do we create the effect of "ad hoc-ism" without handing out the hammers and without having to go through the management.

SPATIAL POSSIBILITIES FOR INTERNAL ISLAND

BUILDINGS INTERSECTION TYPES

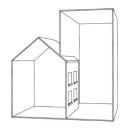

INTERSECTION BECOMES LOW WALL   FAÇADE EXPRESSED ON INTERIOR

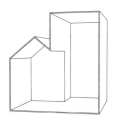

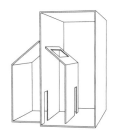

BOTH WALLS REMOVED   INTERSECTION BECOMES CORRIDOR   INTERSECTION BECOMES ROOM

Various building intersection typologies are deployed throughout the site. Several of them are evident within the large center island.

Animating Urbanism: Lasha Brown and Ashima Chitre Due to Bishopsgate Goods Yard's original function as a large piece of urban infrastructure, the question of how someone creates a unique urban experience at such an important intersection of cultures becomes imperative. This project presents a model of how one might begin to approach the problem of designing simultaneously for several different identities.

Taking its cues from the adjacent neighborhoods, our proposal collects programs, urban spaces, circulation typologies, and infrastructures, treats them as found objects, and organizes them on the site to create an urban experience that is thoroughly new while at the same time familiar. We used the remains of the goods-yard viaduct as a framework for stitching together the surrounding neighborhoods, transforming the top of the viaduct into an elevated street with new housing above and commercial programs inserted into the archways below, creating an east-west axis along which all the new cultural and commercial programs and public spaces could be organized.

Two key elements to promote movement across the site are the museum and housing structure on the eastern edge and the elevated street and housing. The roof of the museum is a terraced landscape beginning at Brick Lane and gradually stepping down to seamlessly meet the elevated street. Single-family housing is distributed on the museum's roof, while parking to serve both housing and museum are sandwiched between the terraced roof and the museum's interior volume. The elevated housing consists of four unit types in varying configurations to create an array of different spatial situations. The configurations allow for each unit to face both the elevated street and the units' communal "backyards." Several different design tactics were used throughout this scheme. At midterm we used the technique of bricolage to gather various iconic buildings from around the world and replicate them on our site to form a new arts district. This vision was transformed over the following weeks and developed into a much more complex use of the urban space. The layering of people and program became an important aim as we introduced new user groups to new places by overlaying uses round the site. A theater/auditorium that looks out onto a park over an amphitheater makes a single urban zone in which multiple user groups are able to interact. Our presentation also used the technique of montage to show how these spaces could be inhabited. We made several short videos to illustrate the effects of time and activity on the site. Beginning with a rendering of an empty urban space, we showed people inhabiting the space overtime, animating the urban condition to the beat of music. We also used a narrative of potential activities in the space to carry us deeper into the project. Creating characters and scenarios helped us develop more idiosyncratic pieces for our project. Accepting the complexity of urbanity and understanding that you can inform a city but not determine exactitude was an important realization of this project.

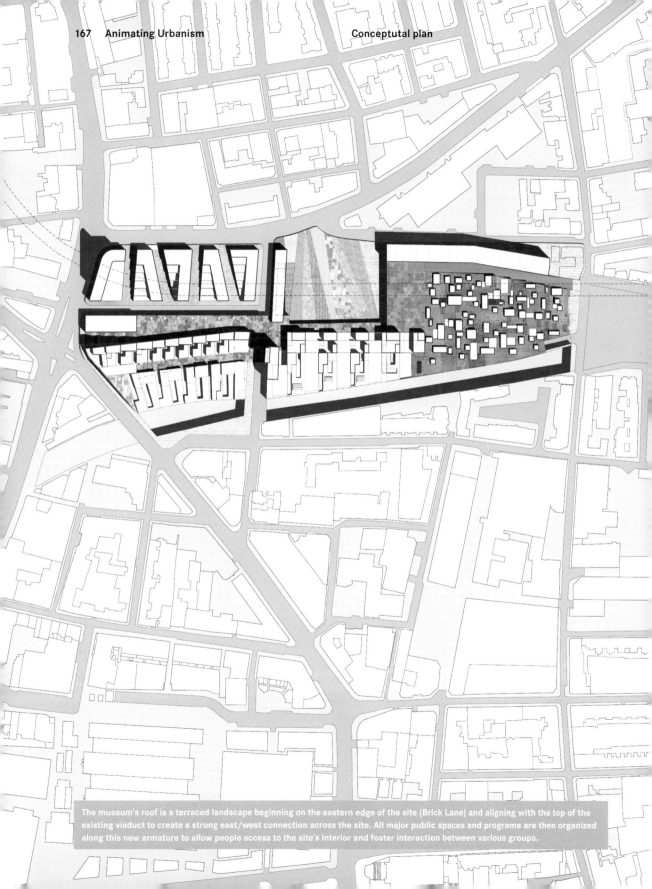

The museum's roof is a terraced landscape beginning on the eastern edge of the site (Brick Lane) and aligning with the top of the existing viaduct to create a strong east/west connection across the site. All major public spaces and programs are then organized along this new armature to allow people access to the site's interior and foster interaction between various groups.

(Above) Figure/ground depiction showing how the proposal relates to the existing fabric. (Opposite) Site movement diagrams show the programs that catalyze movement and how that movement occurs with regard to vehicular and pedestrian flows.

ACTIVATING MOVEMENT

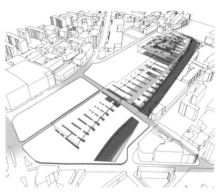

MOVING CARS

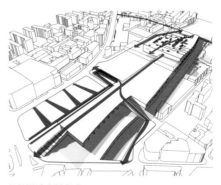

MOVING PEOPLE

Rendering of park view showing access to upper level of existing viaduct.

Emmanuel Petit: Your midterm scheme had a real idea with a campus and all kinds of object buildings, and the public space flowed in-between.

John McMorrough: The key aspect of that scheme was it developed having both the image of "ad hoc-ism" and the ability to add large floor plates and smaller units within the site. The campus gave you both big outdoor and big indoor, and it's a really interesting mix. Now you have inverted what I thought were the qualities of that scheme into something that, for the most part, relies on a model on a very small scale, the accumulation of extremely small-scale, room-scale moves over a very large site. In some moments it could be convincing, but as a pervasive condition it seems like a very intentional move to go small scale—in a much smaller scale than the fabric existing around the site. You didn't do a mat building, but I think you have all the difficulties of a mat in terms of circulation, in terms of frontage, and in terms of access. What is the strategic value of the small-scale model of proliferation?

Susan Yelavich: That is its beauty for me. The idea that it functions as one extremely textured land mass works very well. I like the proliferation and fragmentation. I am curious, does the world need another museum? I don't think the world can support the museums it has already. But on the other hand, the way you've designed it, it doesn't have to be a museum.

Emmanuel Petit: I would say this is a 1960s revision of Modernism that attempts to make it more human, break down the scale, add a little confetti here and there, and have a little pedestrian street so the problem with the cars gets solved.

John McMorrough: I think the house model's proliferation on the hillside is pervasive domesticity within the public realm. It's very different from this campus model with the large-figure buildings being eaten away by the smaller pavilions. For me, the whole notion of the hill doesn't actually partake in its evocation.

Susan Yelavich: Couldn't the rooftops become a rooftop garden to maintain a sense of continuity?

Mimi Zieger: Then it becomes an issue of who gets to use that rooftop.

Frank Lupo: The rooftop could be where everybody gets to do their additions and build-outs of their ideal housing. It appears that it can plug into the central spine of circulation. You have to find your way either up

(Opposite) Rendering showing stair entrance to site from Shoreditch High Street.

on the hill or find your way back down; if you just want to go through, you have to find that path underneath it to get through. In a way it turns its back on everything.

Kieran Long: I like the fact the museum doesn't have a face. I think there's something quite intriguing about that. But it is perverse and weird that the cars get to be on the first floor and the paintings are in the basement. The idea of a new topography in London with public space at high levels and a sense of looking over things would be unusual.

John McMorrough: The value of the project is in its small-scale moves and the accumulation of those bits. I'm wondering, strategically, what instigated that decision?

Lasha Brown: From the midterm review we focused on this question of difference. It made us have a knee-jerk reaction to that question, so we did the small-scale stuff, where everything can have its own voice.

Michael Speaks: The presentation is reflected in the model. It is almost too exquisite to be able to explain anything about itself.

Nick Johnson: I am taken by the playfulness and the romance of this notion of small scale and the really fractured, splintered ground floor on the top of these arches.

Frank Lupo: I like the richness of the sequence it creates in terms of moving through. You might find yourself coming through or over or under this hill town, and then it opens up to this Wailing Wall cut in the middle, which is the almost green space. You possibly would not realize you were one story above before you actually were one story above and looking down into this open green space.

Mimi Zeiger: I am looking for bigger spaces, especially in the museum section and in the parking lot. They seem too petite to serve this scale of a site. Bigger, dumber spaces are what I would like to see, then the delicate pieces could begin to play off the more stupid pieces.

A combination of various architectural sources are montaged onto the site.

A combination of various architectural sources are montaged onto the site.

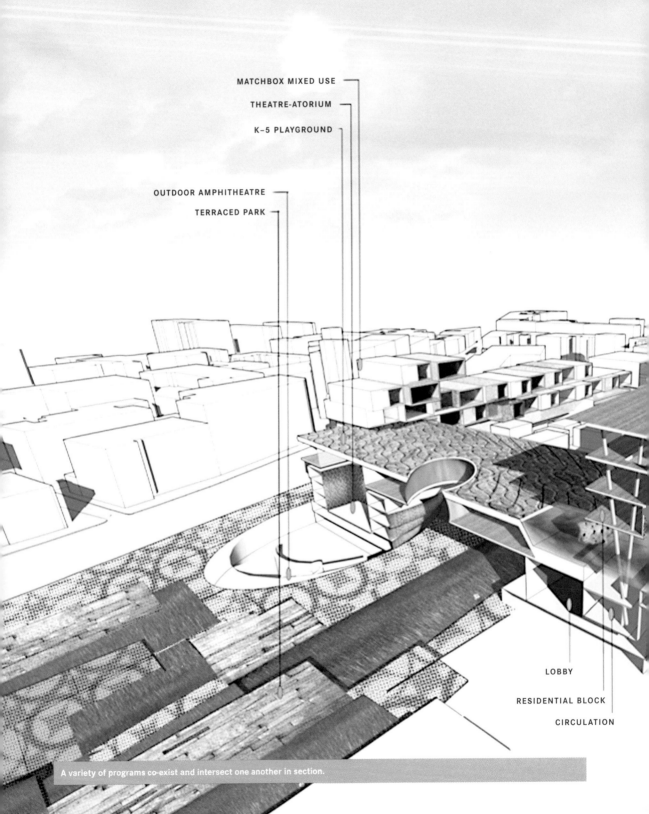

MATCHBOX MIXED USE

THEATRE-ATORIUM

K–5 PLAYGROUND

OUTDOOR AMPHITHEATRE

TERRACED PARK

LOBBY

RESIDENTIAL BLOCK

CIRCULATION

A variety of programs co-exist and intersect one another in section.

UNDERBELLY POOL

GYMNASIUM

HILL TOWN: MULTI FAMILY HOUSING,
WEEKEND MARKET

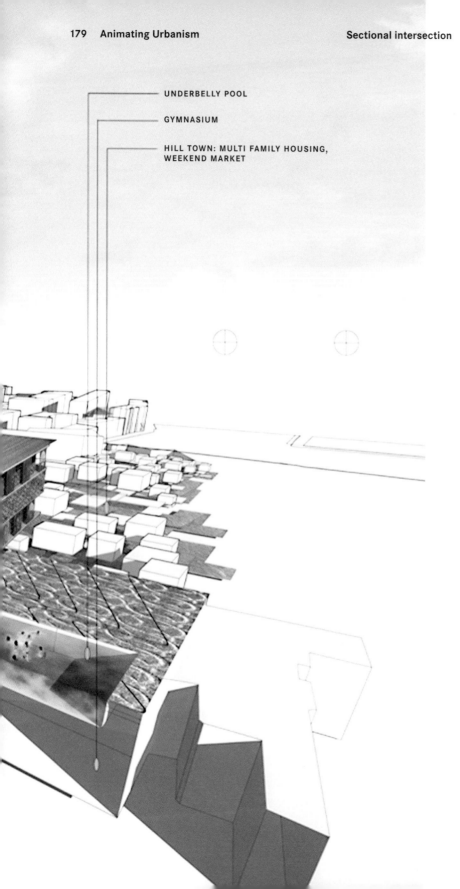

X-100: HOUSES

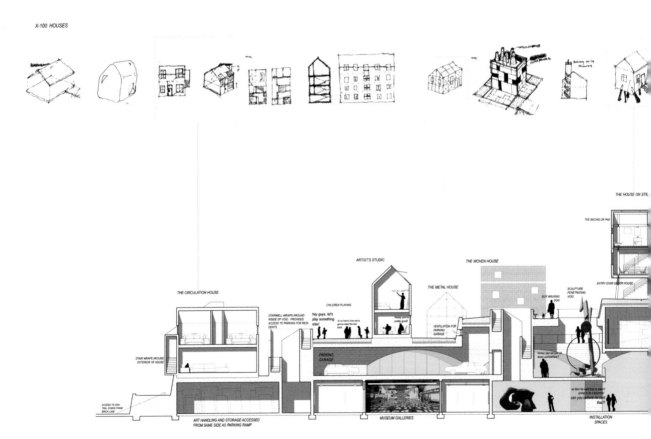

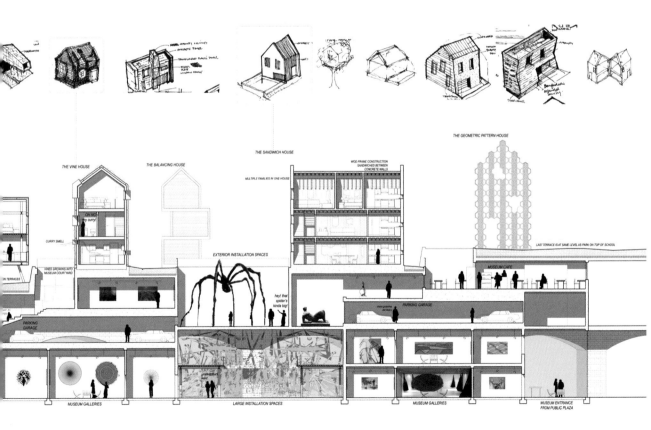

Housing typologies across the site are overlaid onto arts program and underground parking, forming a new type of hill town.

Housing is developed to sit on the museum's terraced roof. The design of the individual units are drawn from some of the vernacular single family homes found in the region.

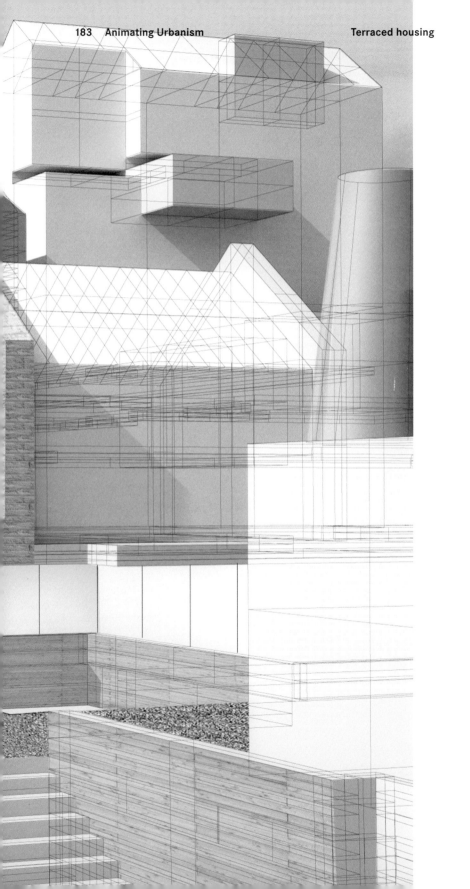

FINAL REVIEWS

SOUTH ELEVATION   WEST ELEVATION

(Opposite) Student Gabrielle Ho, and (above) student Chiemeka Ejioch, present their projects.

Kieran Long: In London, there is no culture of planning or urban-scale thinking at all, and it is hard to have a conversation in London about the urban scale. I would urge you all to go back to London, bring some of these ideas with you, and show them to people.

Frank Lupo: I really appreciated the variety of thought, direction, and some of the audacity in these projects. Initially some ideas might have been off-putting, but once we had the chance to explore them and be taken down the road of logic, one began to perceive there was some real viability in some of these ideas.

Susan Yelavitch: We are irrational, and I like seeing designs that reflect that.

Michael Speaks: One of the things I like a lot about FAT's work is, they challenge conventions. In the first project we saw today, we were looking for a narrative. There's a difference between a narrative and the way you tell the story, as well as the narrative and the way you make the thing.

Emmanuel Petit: I still think it is a problem when architecture turns into a duck—when the way it looks is what is to be communicated. When a building would suddenly look like a cow, that is just over the top. It might turn banal at some point. Those buildings are not dependent on just one metaphor that either gets successfully or unsuccessfully communicated.

Nick Johnson: It has been a really interesting experience for me from the first day in these studios, when we each came in and presented what the studio was going to be about. The studio was fairly free, which also held some risk because we weren't going to condition you. We weren't going to say, "This is what we want from you" or "This is what we expect from you," because we wanted you to be free to think through it for yourselves. It has been an exciting journey because none of us was aware of where we would end up. We found it very stimulating, and obviously it worked for all the critics. It has been a very interesting dialogue and incredibly rewarding.

Sean Griffiths: Nick, has your view changed in terms of what architects do, or do you think architects should do something different than what they do on the basis of what you've seen here? Generally, in this discussion and in other architectural discussions I have heard, a very particular kind of language is used. For example, the word *program*, which everyone else knows as "use," or the word *space*. Only architects and the inhabitants of the *Starship Enterprise* talk about "space." Everyone else talks about "rooms" or "streets."

Nick Johnson: I suppose what I have seen more than I am used to is more abstract and deep intellectual discussions. As you step away from academia and go out and get jobs in the real world, there are fundamentally different issues that affect the discussion. The production of commercial spaces is inherently developer-led. This depth of discussion has been particularly interesting for me. What worries me is, you probably will have very little chance to do that once you are out of school.

Sean Griffiths: That abstraction architects talk about and developers don't talk about, do you see that as having value?

Nick Johnson: The problem with architects, in my view, is that from here on in you will live your lives through architectural crits. Everything is a crit. Every time you put a line on a piece of paper you think about when you went to college and how you had to defend your work. That is inherently a bit of a problem for me because you're always thinking about peer review and about where your project fits into architectural history—that's the slightly unnerving sense I get from the studios. I commend bringing people in from different environments than your immediate peers who know architectural history, who know the detail of the subject of which I, as a non-architect, don't have a strong grasp. The instigation of a school to start that dialogue is quite interesting.

Sam Jacob: Has it changed your view of architects? You were quite suspicious at the beginning of the semester about how architects think about buildings. Do you now understand a bit more about why we do the things that we do?

Nick Johnson: Retaining a healthy skepticism is my job, although my skepticism is far less rigorous than the skepticism that others in my profession reserve for architects.

188

(Clockwise, from top left) Emmanuel Petit, Sean Griffiths, John McMorrough, Kieran Long, Michael Speaks, Charles Holland, Sam Jacob, Susan Yelavich, Patrick Bellew, Frank Lupo, Nick Johnson, Robert A. M. Stern, and Elihu Rubin.

Patrick Bellew is the founding principal of Atelier Ten, environmental engineers based in London and New York City. He has taught at the Bartlett School of Architecture, the University of Reading, and De Montfort University, Leicester, and has been a visiting lecturer at the Yale School of Architecture since 2001. Bellew was elected a fellow of the Royal Academy of Engineering in London in 2004, an honorary fellow of the Royal Institute of British Architects in 2000, and a fellow of the Royal Society of Arts in 1997. He holds a bachelor of science from the School of Architecture and Building Engineering at the University of Bath.

Kieran Long is an architectural journalist, critic, and teacher based in London. Since 2007, he has been the editor of *The Architects' Journal* and was the former deputy editor of *Building Design* and *World Architecture* magazines. He is author of the books *Hatch, The New Architectural Generation* (2008), *New London Interiors* (2004) and co-author of *Architects Today* (2004).

Frank Lupo is an associate principal at FXFowle, where he has worked since 2003. He was part of the design team for residential towers in New York, including Sky House, The Epic, and Three Hudson Boulevard. Previously, Lupo served as director of design at Perkins & Will and was an associate at Skidmore, Owings & Merrill. His work has been published nationally and internationally, and he has participated in several major architectural exhibitions, including *The Un-Private House* at the Museum of Modern Art. Frank received his bachelor of architecture degree from University of Cincinnati and his master of architecture from Yale University. He was the president of the Architectural League of New York from 1998 to 2002.

John McMorrough is an assistant professor of architecture and the architecture graduate studies chairman at Ohio State University's Knowlton School of Architecture. He received a Ph.D. in architecture from Harvard University in 2007, a master of architecture from Harvard University's Graduate School of Design in 1998, and a bachelor of architecture from the University of Kansas in 1992. He is currently principal of StudioAPT in Columbus, Ohio, and has previously worked for OMA/AMO in Rotterdam, Rothman Partner in Boston, Oaklander, Coogan & Vitto Architects in New York, and Ellerbe Becket in Kansas City, Missouri. McMorrough has won several awards for architectural design, lectures extensively, and has a large body of published work. He has taught design studios and seminars at Yale School of Architecture, Massachusetts Institute of Technology, Harvard University Graduate School of Design, and Northeastern University.

Emmanuel Petit is an assistant professor at the Yale School of Architecture, where he teaches architectural design and the history and theory of architecture. He holds a master of architecture from the Swiss Federal Institute of Technology, in Zurich, and both a master of arts and a doctorate in architecture from Princeton University. His essays have appeared in *Log, Thesis, JSAH, Perspecta*, and *Constructs*, among other publications. He is the editor of *Philip Johnson and the Constancy of Change* (Yale University Press, 2009). He has received research grants from The Graham Foundation in the Fine Arts, Griswold research grants from the Whitney Humanities Center at Yale University, a Collection Research Fellowship at The Canadian Centre for Architecture in Montreal, and a European Studies Council Award from Yale's Whitney and Betty McMillan Center for International and Area Studies. In 2003, he co-curated Peter Eisenman's exhibition *Barefoot on White-Hot Walls* at the Museum for Applied Art, in Vienna. As an architectural designer, he has worked for Josef Paul Kleihues, Jean Nouvel, and Peter Eisenman and currently has a practice with Ralitza Petit.

Elihu Rubin was the Daniel Rose ('51) Visiting Assistant Professor of Urbanism at the Yale School of Architecture in 2008–09 and has a Ph.D. in urban planning from the University of California, Berkeley. His research interests focus on nineteenth- and twentieth-century urbanism, cultural landscapes, transportation, social life, and the history and theory of city planning. He has made documentary films on topics relating to urban history, public space, urban redevelopment, and modern architecture.

Michael Speaks is the dean of the College of Design and professor of architecture at the University of Kentucky. He has published and lectured internationally on contemporary art, architecture, urban design, and scenario planning. Former director of the graduate program and founding director of the Metropolitan Research and Design postgraduate program at the Southern California Institute of Architecture in Los Angeles, Speaks also has taught in the graphic design department at the Yale School of Art, as well as in the architecture programs at Harvard University, Columbia University, the University of Michigan, the Berlage Institute, UCLA, Technical University of Delft, and the Art Center College of Design. Speaks is founding editor of the cultural journal *Polygraph*, a former contributing editor of *Any*, and is currently a contributing editor for *Architectural Record*.

Susan Yelavich is an assistant professor at the Parsons School of Constructed Environments, in New York, where she teaches courses in design history and criticism. She was the former assistant director for public programs at Cooper-Hewitt, National Design Museum, where she co-curated the 2003 National Design Triennial. She received her MFA from Cranbrook Academy of Art. She was awarded the Roland Rome Prize Fellowship in Design from the American Academy in Rome in 2003–04. She is author of numerous books including *Contemporary World Interiors* (2006), editor and author of *Pentagram Profile* (2004), co-author of *Inside Design Now* (2003), and author of *Design for Life* (1997) and *The Edge of the Millennium: An*

International Critique of Architecture, Urban Planning, Product, and Communication Design (1993). She is also a contributing editor of *Patek Philippe* magazine.

Frederick Tang is principal of deFT Projects LLC, an architecture firm based in Dumbo, Brooklyn. He has taught at the Columbia Graduate School of Architecture, Planning, and Preservation and the Yale School of Architecture. He was managing editor of *Re-Reading Perspecta: The First Fifty Years of the Yale Architecture Journal* (MIT Press, 2005) and is currently a project editor for *PRAXIS Journal*.

Mimi Zeiger is a contributing writer for *Architect* magazine and author of *New Museums: Contemporary Museum Architecture Around the World* (Universe 2005) and *Tiny Houses* (Rizzoli 2009). She is editor and publisher of *loud paper,* a zine dedicated to increasing the volume of architectural discourse. The publication received grant awards from the Graham Foundation for the Arts and the LEF Foundation. She has written for *Dwell, Azure,* and *Metropolis* magazines and a catalog essay on Andrea Zittel for the Goetz Collection. She has taught at the California College of the Arts and at the Southern California Institute of Architecture on the relationships among architecture, art, urban space, and popular culture. She holds a master of architecture from SCI-Arc and a bachelor of architecture from Cornell University.

Image credits Andrei Harwell: 72–73, 184–185, 188; Ashima Chitre: 88–89, 96–97, 108–111, 113, 167–169, 178–181; Brandt Knapp: 13; Chiemeka Ejiochi: 115–118, 120, 122–123; Christina Wu: 59–69, fold-out, 76, 85, 153–162, 165; Christopher Corbett: cover, 104–105, 126, 129–132; Elizabeth McDonald: 87, 102–103, 112–113, 139–143, 150; FAT: 19, 26–29, 36–37; Frans Barten: 18–19; Gabrielle Ho: fold-out, 76, 81–83, 153, 154–162, 165; *Illustrated London News:* 53; Lasha Brown: fold-out, 98–99, 113, 167–172, 174–177, 182–183; Lydia Miller: 56, 86, 90–93, 101, 125, 129, 134–137; mgmt design: 56; Nicholas McDermott: 59–69, 78–79, 94–95, 106–107, 112–113, 139, 140–144, 147, 149; Office of National Statistics (www.statistics.gov.uk): 56; Paul Dunn: 50, 70–71; Phil Gyford (www.gyford.com): 50; Shelley Zhang: 115–18, 120; Subterranea Britannica (www.subbrit.org.uk): 54–55; Tim Soar: 38, 40–41; Urban Splash: 12, 16, 32–33; Will Alsop Partners: 22–23